Cooking with Japanese Pickles

97 Quick, Classic and Seasonal Recipes

Takako Yokoyama

TUTTLE Publishing

Tokyo | Rutland, Vermont | Singapore

Contents

Why I Wrote This Book

I grew up in the mountainous region of Shinshu (the old name for what is now Nagano prefecture), and I have eaten many kinds of traditional Japanese pickles since I was a child. Pickles were not only served with every meal, but were even eaten with tea. They were all homemade by my mother. I have been familiar with those flavors, and studied the techniques for creating them, all my life. A vegetable will take on a different flavor and character depending on how it's pickled—in salt, in rice bran, in vinegar.

In Shinshu, vegetables cannot be grown during the long winters. Therefore, preserving the vegetables that are harvested in the summer and fall so that they last a long time has always been a way of life there. One method for accomplishing this is pickling. Our ancestors' knowledge of how to provide variety for our tables in this manner forms the foundation for our lives to this day.

When I make pickles, I feel the changing of the seasons so intimately. In the spring I go excitedly to the mountains to gather fresh wild shoots and capture their fragrance in jars. In the summer, I buy mountains of vegetables and turn them into pickles for the colder months. And from late fall onward, I make barrels full of pickles to last until the coming spring.

As I continue to preserve vegetables in these ways, new ideas for making them even more delicious spring to my mind, and my pickles continue to evolve. This book is filled with my tips and ideas for making tasty pickles of your own.

Traditional Japanese pickles are great fun to make at home, and they're something you'll look forward to eating at any time. Give some of these recipes a try, and welcome new kinds of pickles into your life!

—**Takako Yokoyama**

The Merits of Making Your Own Pickles

- Pickles use ingredients that are easy to obtain in season.

- Pickling makes vegetables delicious and easy to eat in quantity.

- Pickled vegetables are very nutritious, with plenty of beneficial lactic-acid bacteria, vitamins, minerals and fiber.

- Homemade pickles contain no artificial preservatives.

- You can taste the seasons in your pickles—and they're fun to make, too!

Pickles are nutritious and delicious: The secret is fermentation

The vegetables used to make pickles contain many elements that keep our bodies in good working order, such as vitamins, minerals and dietary fiber. In addition, pickles make great use of the power of fermentation.

In salt pickling and rice-bran pickling, fermentation progresses due to the salt used, which increases the lactic acid bacteria and imparts a sour taste to the vegetables. These microorganisms are thought to be highly beneficial for health; they help to keep the digestive system in good order, and may even increase immunity. Vegetables that are pickled in soy sauce, miso or sake lees also absorb nutrients from those ingredients, as well as the benefits of koji mold (*Aspergillus oryzae* or *A. sojae*) that they contain, making the pickles even more nutritious.

Pickles, then, are an excellent source of nutrition, and are quite healthy. Some people may be concerned about the amount of salt they contain, but as long as you use the correct amount of salt to make your pickles, this should not be a concern. It is also believed that the potassium in pickled vegetables helps to eliminate excess sodium from the body.

Why do pickles taste so good? As mentioned, in salt-pickled vegetables, the salt encourages the growth of lactic-acid bacteria, and the sour taste that the pickles develop makes them delicious. In the case of pickles made with ingredients that contain koji mold—such as soy sauce, miso or sake lees—the koji ferments to create a beneficial yeast called *kobo*, which increases the umami of the vegetables. You might say that the delicious taste of pickles is the taste of fermentation. Since this is a slow, leisurely process, you can enjoy a slightly different level of sourness and umami with each batch of pickles you make.

Adding homemade pickles to your table every day lets you enjoy their great flavor and gain health benefits at the same time. That's a win-win!

The joy of pickling with the seasons

Even in my home region of Shinshu, where it used to be impossible to grow vegetables in winter, these days the development of heated greenhouses and refrigeration facilities has made all kinds of vegetables available year round. This is a very agricultural area, so there are a lot of vegetable varieties available. Believe it or not, the residents of Nagano prefecture consume more vegetables than

anyone else in Japan. Perhaps it's because they like pickles so much—that's what I like to think, anyway.

Even though vegetables may be available year-round, for pickling it's best to use vegetables in season. If you select fresh, sweet vegetables for your pickles, they'll have the best flavor and the greatest nutritional value.

In order to obtain vegetables in peak season, I often go to a roadside farmer's market that's a little far from where I live. I don't mind the trip, though; the fields and rice paddies I pass along the way as I drive on back roads to get to the farmer's market, the sound of water as it rushes through the streams, and the flowers in bloom on the sides of hills and mountains all make the journey a pleasure.

Making pickles also heightens the awareness of the changing of the seasons. In the eagerly awaited early spring I start to wonder whether certain wild plants are emerging, or whether I should go out and dig for young, tender bamboo shoots. Every day contains excitement and anticipation. In the summer, I usually put up about 220 pounds (100 kilograms) of umeboshi (salt-preserved ume fruit), which is pretty tough work physically. Even in the winter, I keep an eye out for when the local leafy mustard green called *nozawana* has been turned sweet and tender by frost. I'm also busy ordering the supplies needed to dry and pickle daikon radishes to make *takuan*.

Even with all that work to do, I've never gotten sick, perhaps because I'm always eating healthy, delicious pickles. I feel gratitude from the bottom of my heart for being able to continue to live the pickling life, season after season and year after year.

Pickling Equipment

Containers

Since pickles are both salty and acidic, it's important to use containers that are nonreactive. Metal containers, especially uncoated cast iron, should not be used, as they may become corroded.

The white containers shown above are heat-resistant enamel containers with enamel lids. The enamel, which is made from ground glass, protects the core metal material and does not absorb any odors, making them ideal as containers for pickling beds (e.g., the rice-bran pickles on page 37) as well as for storing pickles. Watch out for chips, which can lead to corrosion.

If enameled containers aren't available, a good substitute is sturdy glass ovenware with matching lids—preferably also glass. Plastic lids can absorb odors, but they may be used, and replaced as needed. Glass lets in light, which may not be desirable for an active pickling bed. If you use glass, keep the container in a dark location or cover it with an air-permeable dark cloth that allows the contents to breathe, but blocks light.

Ceramic containers are very attractive (shown above are examples from the author's collection); they are also nonreactive, which means they are ideal for making or storing many types of pickles. Ceramic ovenware works well; you can look for suitable containers at flea markets and thrift shops. The jar shown above left is a classic pickling jar with a lid. It has a capacity of about 2 quarts (2 liters), a good size for making a variety of pickles.

Glass jars, like the two shown bottom right, are ideal for pickling when you want to be able to observe the contents as they mature. A container like the tall, slender one shown here is great for pickles with a lot of liquid.

Mixing bowls

Glass bowls are ideal for mixing together pickle ingredients, since they are nonreactive. Ceramic bowls work well, too. In some cases, a bowl can be used as is with a weight on top to make pickles right in it.

Scales

Pickling is a science; all the ingredients should be measured by weight, not volume, for the best results. The old manual scale shown here is used by the author to weigh vegetables; the more precise digital scale is used for seasonings and the like.

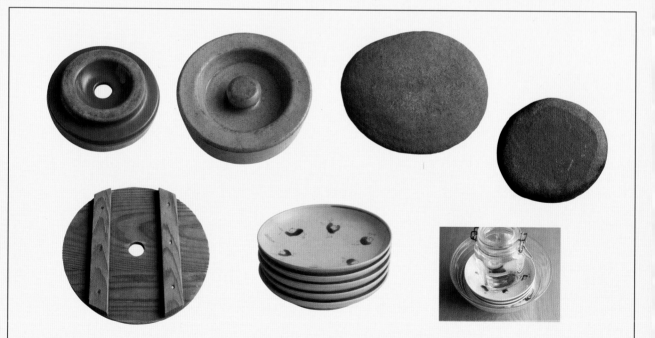

Weights

Some pickles call for a weight to be set on them as they mature. Like pickling containers, these fermentation weights should be made of a nonreactive material in case they come in contact with the pickles.

The round fermentation weights shown here are ceramic, and are designed to fit into jars. You can also use stones, but they must be carefully cleaned and weighed beforehand to confirm that you are using the correct weight for the job.

You can make an improvised weight by placing a jar full of water, or a bag of flour, rice, beans, etc., on a ceramic plate, then setting the plate on top of the pickles. Be sure to weigh everything first so that you are adding the weight called for in the recipe. Protect the weight from moisture by placing it in a sealed plastic bag.

The round wooden disc shown here is called a drop lid. It is set on top of the pickles before the weight is added so that the weight is evenly distributed. A plate small enough to fit inside the container can be used for this purpose.

Glossary of Ingredients

The secret to making delicious pickles is to use the best possible ingredients, free of preservatives or additives. Use pure salt that is non-iodized, and use sugar that is minimally processed. Choose vinegar, soy sauce and mirin that contain no additives, and miso that has been fermented for some time. Good ingredients that have been made with care really bring out the best flavors in vegetables. The Japanese ingredients listed here can be bought online or found at well-stocked Japanese grocery stores.

Abura-age
Thin rectangles of deep-fried tofu available at Japanese grocery stores, often in the freezer section. Deep-fried "tofu puffs," available at Asian or Chinese grocery stores, are similar and can be substituted.

Bamboo shoots

Bamboo shoots can be found fresh, vacuum-packed or canned at Asian grocery stores. Most packaged and canned bamboo shoots are pre-boiled.

Beni-shoga
This pink or magenta shredded ginger is pickled in the salty-sour liquid produced from making umeboshi. Available at Japanese or general Asian grocery stores. (Not to be confused with *gari*, the pale-pink or tan pickled ginger slices eaten with sushi.)

Bonito flakes
Called *katsuobushi* in Japanese, these are thinly shaved flakes of fermented, dried and aged skipjack tuna or bonito. Bonito flakes are an essential ingredient in Japanese cooking, used to make dashi stock and also as a garnish. Available at Japanese grocery stores or online.

Burdock root

You may be able to find burdock root, known as *gobo* in Japan, at an Asian grocery store.

Chinese yam
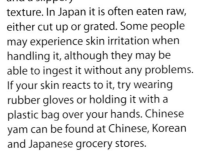
This root vegetable, called *nagaimo* in Japanese, has pale-brown skin and a slippery texture. In Japan it is often eaten raw, either cut up or grated. Some people may experience skin irritation when handling it, although they may be able to ingest it without any problems. If your skin reacts to it, try wearing rubber gloves or holding it with a plastic bag over your hands. Chinese yam can be found at Chinese, Korean and Japanese grocery stores.

Chrysanthemum flowers
You may be able to find small edible chrysanthemum flowers in Japanese grocery stores, where they are often sold as a garnish for sushi and sashimi. If not, you may be able to grow an edible variety from seed.

Daikon radish

A thick white root vegetable with a spicy flavor and crunchy texture when raw. When cooked, it becomes tender and sweet. One of the most popular vegetables in Japan, it can be found in Asian grocery stores as well as many regular supermarkets.

Eggplant
Japanese eggplants are slender with thin skin, and are readily available at Japanese grocery stores. Chinese eggplant (widely available at Asian markets) or mini Italian or Indian varieties may be substituted.

Karashi mustard powder
Available at Japanese or Asian grocery stores and often labeled "Oriental Hot Mustard."

Kiriboshi daikon
These dried daikon radish strips are available at Japanese grocery stores.

Kombu seaweed

Kombu is a leathery seaweed that is used dried as a rich source of umami flavor. It is available in many forms: as whole leaves, squares, or shredded. It is available at Asian grocery stores and online.

Lotus root
Lotus root can be found fresh at Asian markets. It is also sometimes sold pre-cooked in pouches.

Mirin

Mirin is a sweet liquor made by fermenting short-grain sweet rice with rice koji, mixing it with a distilled liquor called *shochu* and aging it for about 2 months. Make sure to use the type labeled *hon mirin*, which means "real mirin," and not additive-laden *aji mirin* or "mirin seasoning."

Miso paste

Miso is a flavorful paste of soybeans fermented with microorganisms from rice koji. Use miso that contains only soybeans, rice koji and salt, without any preservatives or other additives.

Mochi rice cake

Glutinous rice is steamed and then pounded until smooth to make a cake that becomes crispy on the outside and chewy on the inside when toasted. Available at natural food stores, Japanese grocery stores or online, in a dried, shelf-stable form.

Myoga ginger

Myoga ginger buds have a mildly pungent flavor. You may be able to find them at well-stocked Japanese grocery stores. If you can't find them, use young ginger shoots or sliced singer root instead.

Natto

These slightly bitter, very gooey fermented soybeans are usually sold frozen at Asian grocery stores.

Rice koji

Rice koji is steamed rice that has been inoculated with the *Aspergillus oryzae* mold. It's used to make all kinds of fermented foods in Japan, including sake, miso paste and soy sauce. You can find it in dry or fresh form at Asian markets or online. It is also referred to in English as "malted rice."

Rice vinegar

Rice vinegar is a mild, clear-flavored vinegar. Try to find one made only with rice, without distilled alcohol added.

Sake

Use a sake that you can drink, rather than one labeled "cooking sake," which contains additives.

Sake lees

Sake lees (*sake kasu* in Japanese) are the parts of fermented rice that are left over after the sake is squeezed out. There are two types: one that comes in sheets, and a paste as shown here. For making pickles, a well-matured paste type is the best. Sake lees can be found at Japanese grocery stores or online. If there's a sake brewery in your area, you may be able to obtain some directly.

Salt

For all the pickling recipes in this book you will get best results with a non-iodized salt such as pure sea salt with no additives, or kosher salt. When making pickles, it's extremely important to weigh the vegetables and measure the amount of salt so that the ratios are correct.

Sardines, dried

Whole small dried sardines, called *niboshi* in Japanese are used in various dishes and soups for their umami, instead of or in addition to kombu seaweed. If you can, choose a type that has no added salt. They are available at Japanese grocery stores and online.

Shiso leaves and berries

Shiso (*Perilla frutescens* var. *crispa*) is an herb used extensively in Japanese cooking. There are two main types: green, which has bright green leaves; and red, with dark red-purple leaves. The red variety is slightly bitter; green shiso is mild enough to use fresh in salad. Both types of leaf as well as shiso berries can be found in well-stocked Japanese grocery stores, but it may be easier to grow your own from seeds, often sold in the ornamental-plant section of seed catalogs.

Soy sauce

Two types of soy sauce are used in this book. One is dark soy sauce, ideally made with organic ingredients—soybeans, wheat and salt—and no preservatives. Light soy sauce has a lighter color and is best when you want to preserve the colors of the vegetables you are pickling.

Sugar

For the recipes in this book raw (unrefined) cane sugar with large crystals is recommended.

Ume fruit

The fruits of the ume tree (*Prunus mume*) are often referred to as plums, but they are actually a type of apricot. Ume are very sour even when ripe, and need to be pickled or preserved in salt or sugar to become edible.

Ripe ume are available at well-stocked Japanese or Korean grocery stores for a short period when they are in season (usually in June in the northern hemisphere). You may also be able to buy them online.

Wasabi leaves

You may be able to find wasabi leaves at farmers' markets, or you can try growing your own from seed.

Yuzu citrus

This Japanese citrus fruit has a distinct sharp flavor. It is periodically available fresh at Japanese or Korean groceries. If you find a fresh yuzu, buy it, remove the zest and juice and freeze for later use. Yuzu juice and yuzu salt are available online. Limes, lemons, grapefruits or a combination of all three can be used as substitutes in recipes.

CHAPTER 1

Quick Pickles

Quick pickles are great when you want to add one more item to your
dinner menu at the last minute. They're simple, fast and delicious.
Most of the pickles in this chapter can be made in as little as 30 minutes,
or overnight at the most. They have fresh, bright salad-like flavors
and textures that bring out the best in the vegetables.
The brief pickling heightens the flavor.

Since the pickling process reduces the volume of the vegetables,
you can eat quite a lot of them, and since no oil is used they are very
low in fat. All of the recipes are for amounts that are easy to make,
so you can try them all and discover your favorite!

Eggplant Pickled in Salt

Pickling the eggplants in brine helps them retain their texture. Adding an iron fish to the brine gives the skins a bright color. These refreshing pickles are especially nice in the heat of summer.

3 small Asian eggplants, about 8 oz (240 g) total
½ teaspoon salt

FOR THE PICKLING BRINE
4 cups (1 liter) water
3½ oz (100 g) salt
Iron cooking fish or ball

Container capacity: 8½ cups (2 liters)
Pickling time: 8 hours
Lifespan: 3 days refrigerated

* In the brine, the iron cooking fish or ball will turn the eggplant skins a beautiful color. Make sure the fish is clean and free of rust. You can also use 10 or so old iron nails (new nails may have a chemical coating, so they should not be used). Save and reuse the pickling brine if you wish.

1 Cut the eggplants in half lengthwise, leaving the calyxes intact. Rub the salt into the cut sides.

2 Mix up the brine in a bowl. Put the iron fish in the bottom of the pickling vessel and add half the brine.

3 Add the eggplants and pour the rest of the brine over.

4 Put a 1 pound (500 g) weight on top to keep the eggplants submerged. Let stand for 8 hours at room temperature. Remove the eggplants from the brine and store in the refrigerator.

Turnips Pickled in Salt

Small Asian or baby turnips have a high water content, so they absorb salt very quickly. If you want to speed up the pickling process even more, use a heavy weight on top. Enjoy the green tops if you have them too.

5 small Asian turnips or baby turnips with greens attached, about 1 lb 9 oz (750 g)
2½ teaspoons salt

Container capacity: 12 cups (3 liters)
Pickling time: 30 minutes to 1 hour
Lifespan: 3 days refrigerated

1 Cut off the turnip greens, leaving a bit of stem attached to the roots. Peel the turnip roots and cut each one into 16 segments.

2 Cut the turnip greens into 1 inch (2.5 cm) lengths and sprinkle with 1 teaspoon of the salt. Massage and rub the greens with the salt until they are wilted. Squeeze out the excess moisture.

3 Put the turnip wedges and greens in a bowl. Sprinkle the remaining 1½ teaspoons of salt over all and rub it in well.

4 Place a 3½ pound (1.5 kg) weight on top and let stand at room temperature for 30 minutes to an hour. Refrigerate until serving.

Cabbage Pickled in Salt

Since the leaves are fibrous, shred the cabbage thinly so that it releases moisture easily when salted. Both red and green cabbage may be prepared the same way. Add dressing to this pickled cabbage to turn it into a delicious salad or coleslaw.

½ green or red cabbage, about 14 oz (400 g)
I heaping teaspoon salt (2% of the weight of the cabbage)

Container capacity: 6½ cups (1.5 liters)
Pickling time: 1 hour
Lifespan: 3 days refrigerated

1 Weigh the cabbage so that you can determine the correct amount of salt. Shred the cabbage very finely.

2 Put the shredded cabbage in a bowl and sprinkle with the salt. Massage and squeeze to distribute salt well.

3 Place a 3½ pound (1.5 kg) weight on top of the cabbage and let stand at room temperature for 1 hour. Store in the refrigerator until serving.

Cut Greens Pickled in Salt

Dark leafy greens are pickled by squeezing them with a little salt, then marinating them overnight in seasonings. In Nagano we make this with a vegetable called *nozawana*, but you can make it with komatsuna greens, mustard greens or Swiss chard.

2 lbs (1 kg) dark leafy greens such as komatsuna, mustard greens, Swiss chard or nozawana
3⅓ teaspoons salt (2% of the weight of the greens)
2 tablespoons cane sugar
1 tablespoon soy sauce
2 tablespoons mirin

1 tablespoon + 1 teaspoon rice vinegar
Chopped red chili pepper, to taste

Container capacity: 12 cups (3 liters)
Pickling time: 8 hours
Lifespan: 1 week refrigerated

1 Remove any roots and weigh the greens to determine the correct amount of salt.

2 Cut the greens into 1 inch (2.5 cm) pieces. Put into a bowl and sprinkle with the salt, squeezing lightly to mix.

3 Add the sugar, soy sauce, mirin, vinegar and red chili pepper. Massage the seasonings in well.

4 Place a sturdy plate or lid on top of the greens and put a 6½ pound (3 kg) weight on the plate. Let stand at room temperature for 8 hours. Store in the refrigerator until serving.

Miso-pickled Burdock

You don't need to make a miso pickling bed for this recipe. The burdock root is simply marinated in a small amount of miso that enhances the crunchy texture and fresh flavor. The key here is to parboil the burdock root so that the miso flavor really sinks in.

4½ oz (130 g) burdock root (available at Asian grocery stores)
1 tablespoon miso paste

Container capacity: 2 cups (500 ml)
Pickling time: 8 hours
Lifespan: 5 days refrigerated

1 Wash the burdock root well and cut into 3 inch (7 cm) lengths. Cut each piece lengthwise in half or into quarters. Bring a pan of water to a boil; add the burdock root and parboil for about a minute. Drain.

2 While still hot, place the burdock in a bowl and add the miso. Mix well to combine.

3 Cover and let stand at room temperature for 8 hours. Store in the refrigerator until serving. Eat as is, miso and all.

Miso-pickled Chinese Yam

Chinese yam, called *nagaimo* in Japanese, is a long starchy root that can be eaten raw as well as cooked. The crunchy texture is a great match for the rich taste of miso. Eat soon after making, as they can turn watery if left too long.

**4½ oz (130 g) Chinese yam
(available at Asian grocers)**
1 tablespoon miso paste

Container capacity: 2 cups (500 ml)
Pickling time: 8 hours
Lifespan: 3 days refrigerated

1 Peel the yam and cut into ¾ inch (2 cm) cubes.

2 Place the yam cubes in a bowl and add the miso. Mix well to coat the yam with the miso.

3 Cover and let stand at room temperature for 8 hours. Store in the refrigerator until serving. Eat as is, miso and all.

Miso-pickled Shiitake Mushrooms

Dried shiitake mushrooms have a lot of concentrated umami flavor. Here they are simmered before being covered with miso. These pickles can be eaten mixed with fresh vegetables, added to plain rice, or eaten on their own.

5 dried shiitake mushrooms
½ tablespoon miso paste

Container capacity: 1¼ cups (300 ml)
Pickling time: 8 hours
Lifespan: 5 days refrigerated

1 Soak the dried shiitake mushrooms in water to cover until rehydrated. Cut off the stems. Bring some water to a boil in a pan, add the mushrooms and simmer for 5 minutes. Drain the mushroom caps, then spread a little miso on the inside of each cap.
2 Layer the mushrooms in a small container. Cover and let stand at room temperature for 8 hours. Refrigerate until serving. Cut into thin slices before eating, miso and all.

Miso-pickled Kombu Seaweed

Here, strips of kombu seaweed coated with miso are rolled up tight for pickling, making one great-tasting morsel with two great sources of umami. Cut the rolls into slices and serve as appetizers or accompaniments to drinks, or add to soup as a garnish.

Two 3 x 6 inch (7.5 x 15 cm) strips
kombu seaweed, soaked in water
until soft; or use kombu left over
after making dashi stock
1 tablespoon miso paste

Container capacity: 1 cup (240 ml)
Lifespan: 5 days refrigerated
Pickling time: 8 hours

1 Pat the kombu seaweed strips dry and spread the miso over one side. Roll one strip up tightly. Place the first roll on the edge of the second strip and roll up tightly.
2 Place the roll seam-side–down in a small container. Cover and let stand for 8 hours at room temperature. Store in the refrigerator and slice before serving.

Miso-pickled Bell Peppers

Sweet bell peppers are "cooked" without heat by coating them with miso and letting them sit for a while. Raw vegetables are so easy to eat this way! Enjoy their crisp texture, too.

1 large red bell pepper
1 large yellow bell pepper
1 small green pepper
1 tablespoon miso paste

Container capacity: 2 cups (500 ml)
Pickling time: 8 hours
Lifespan: 3 days refrigerated

1 Cut the bell peppers in half vertically, remove calyxes and seeds, and cut lengthwise into thin slices. Place the peppers in a bowl and add the miso.

2 Mix well to coat the peppers with the miso.

3 Cover and let stand at room temperature for 8 hours. Refrigerate before serving. Eat as is, miso and all.

Cucumber in Soy Sauce and Vinegar

These pickles have the irresistible fragrance of garlic oil and the tang of vinegar. They make a great accompaniment to fish and meat dishes!

2 small Japanese cucumbers or 1 large thin-skinned cucumber, 7 oz (200 g) total
1 garlic clove, finely minced
½ tablespoon rapeseed or canola oil
1 tablespoon light (usukuchi) soy sauce
1 tablespoon rice vinegar

Container capacity: 4 cups (1 liter)
Pickling time: 1 hour
Lifespan: 3 days refrigerated

1 Place a skillet over low heat and add the oil and garlic. Stir-fry the garlic, being careful not to let it burn.

2 Cut the cucumber into chunks (if the seeds are large and watery, remove them) and place in a bowl. Add the garlic and oil while still hot.

3 Add the soy sauce and vinegar and mix to coat the cucumber.

4 Place a 1 pound 3 ounce (600 g) weight on the cucumbers and let stand for 1 hour at room temperature. Store in the refrigerator until serving.

Napa Cabbage in Ginger Soy Sauce

No salt is used in this recipe. Instead, garlic and soy sauce are rubbed into the cabbage to blend with its inherent sweetness. Be sure to use the correct weight to press the cabbage so that it wilts and softens.

¼ large napa cabbage, about 1 lb 3 oz (600 g) total
3 tablespoons light (usukuchi) soy sauce
1 teaspoon grated garlic

Container capacity: 8½ cups (2 liters)
Pickling time: 8 hours
Lifespan: 3 days refrigerated

1 Cut the napa cabbage into approximately 1 inch (2.5 cm) long pieces. Place in a bowl and add the grated garlic.

2 Add the soy sauce.

3 Mix up the contents of the bowl, squeezing the soy sauce into the cabbage with your hands.

4 Set a 4½ pound (2 kg) weight on top and let stand at room temperature for about 8 hours. Store in the refrigerator until serving.

Leeks Pickled in Soy Sauce

The leek's pungency is transformed into umami by the soy sauce! Serve as a side, or as a dipping sauce for hot pots. If you can't find Japanese or Asian leeks, use regular leeks with the tougher outer layers discarded, or green onions.

1 Japanese or Asian leek (naganegi), about 7 oz (200 g)
3 tablespoons soy sauce

Container capacity: 2 cups (500 ml)
Pickling time: 1 hour
Lifespan: 1 week refrigerated

1 Slice the leeks crosswise into thin rings and place in a bowl. Add the soy sauce and mix well to combine.
2 Transfer to a container, cover with a lid, and refrigerate for 1 hour. Keep refrigerated until serving.

Pickled Lettuce

The double umami punch of bonito flakes and dried baby sardines called *chirimenjako* (available in Japanese grocery stores) turns lettuce into a substantial dish. The overnight pickling time really allows the flavors to mingle.

1 head iceberg lettuce, about 14 oz (400 g), cut in half vertically and cored
Handful dried baby sardines, about ⅓ oz (10 g)
½ cup (5 g) bonito flakes
2 tablespoons light (usukuchi) soy sauce
2 tablespoons sake

Container capacity: 12 cups (3 liters)
Pickling time: 8 hours
Lifespan: 3 days refrigerated

1 Place the lettuce halves in a bowl with the cut sides up. Sprinkle the baby sardines over, then follow up with the bonito flakes, so that the cut edges of the lettuce are covered. Swirl the soy sauce and sake over all.
2 Set a 2½ pound (1.2 kg) weight on top and leave for 8 hours. Refrigerate until serving.

Lotus Root and Sardine Pickles

Dried immature sardines called *niboshi* are often used in Japan to make dashi stock. Here, the lotus root soaks up their flavor along with soy sauce. No weight is used, so the lotus roots retain their crunchy texture.

1 segment lotus root, about 5 oz (150 g)
1 tablespoon light (usukuchi) soy sauce
⅓ oz (10 g) dried sardines (niboshi)
1 tablespoon water

Container capacity: 2 cups (500 ml)
Pickling time: 1 hour
Lifespan: 3 days refrigerated

1 Peel the lotus root and slice thinly on a mandoline. Bring a pan of water to a boil. Add the lotus root slices and boil for 1 to 2 minutes. Drain.

2 Transfer the lotus root to a bowl while still hot. Add the water and dried sardines, then swirl in the soy sauce. Mix everything together well.

3 Cover and refrigerate for an hour. Keep refrigerated until serving.

Red Onion Pickled in Sweet Vinegar

The sweet pickling vinegar tones down the sharp bite of the onions. Mix these pickles into salads or serve alongside deep-fried dishes. Their refreshing flavor makes a great foil for rich food.

1 or 2 red onions, about 7 oz (200 g) total

FOR THE SWEET VINEGAR
2 tablespoons rice vinegar
2 tablespoons plus 2 teaspoons water
1 tablespoon sugar
Generous ½ teaspoon salt

Container capacity: 2 cups (500 ml)
Pickling time: 1 hour
Lifespan: 5 days refrigerated

1 Combine the sweet vinegar ingredients in a bowl. Mix well until the sugar and salt are dissolved.

2 Cut the onion in half from pole to pole and slice thinly.

3 Pack the onion into a container so the slices are lying flat.

4 Pour the sweet vinegar over the onion in the container. Cover and refrigerate for 1 hour. Keep refrigerated until serving.

Cauliflower Pickled in Sweet Vinegar

Cauliflower doesn't fall apart after cooking, so it's perfect for pickling. It matches well with sweet vinegar, too. This is a filling dish on its own.

⅓ **head cauliflower, about 7 oz**
(200 g)

FOR THE SWEET VINEGAR
4 tablespoons rice vinegar
⅓ cup (80 ml) water
2 tablespoons sugar
1 heaping teaspoon salt

Container capacity: 3⅓ cups
(800 ml)
Pickling time: 1 hour
Lifespan: 5 days refrigerated

1 Combine the sweet vinegar ingredients in a bowl. Mix well until the sugar and salt are dissolved.

2 Divide the cauliflower into florets. Set a steamer basket over water in a pan and bring to a boil. Add the cauliflower, cover and steam for 5 minutes.

3 Transfer the hot cauliflower to a container and spoon the sweet vinegar over.

4 Cover and leave at room temperature for 1 hour, or until the cauliflower has absorbed the sweet vinegar flavor. Store in the refrigerator until serving.

Potato Pickled in Sweet Vinegar

This is a variation on a traditional pickle served on special occasions in my home region of Shinshu. Potatoes are thinly shredded so that they soak up the flavors of the sweet vinegar. These pickles have a light, airy texture.

2 potatoes, about 10 oz (300 g) total
1 tablespoon canola oil

FOR THE SWEET VINEGAR
2 tablespoons rice vinegar
2 tablespoons plus 2 teaspoons water
1 tablespoon sugar
1 teaspoon salt
1 small red chili pepper, sliced into thin rounds

Container capacity: 8½ cups (2 L)
Pickling time: 30 minutes
Lifespan: 3 days refrigerated

1 Peel the potatoes and cut into very thin matchsticks. Place in a bowl of cold water to rinse off the surface starch, then drain. Repeat this 3 times. Combine the sweet vinegar ingredients and mix well until the sugar and salt are dissolved.

2 Heat the oil in a skillet. Add the well-drained potatoes to the pan and stir-fry slowly over medium-low heat.

3 Transfer the potatoes to a bowl while still hot and pour the sweet vinegar over. Add the red chili pepper and mix well.

4 Place a 2 pound (1 kg) weight on top and let stand at room temperature for about 30 minutes, until the potatoes have soaked up the sweet vinegar. Refrigerate until serving.

Celery in Sweet Vinegar

Celery is left for a short time in sweet vinegar to make a crisp and crunchy pickle. Daikon radish and carrots can be pickled in the same way.

1 celery stalk, about 5 oz (150 g)

FOR THE SWEET VINEGAR
2 tablespoons rice vinegar
2 tablespoons plus 2 teaspoons water
1 tablespoon sugar
1 teaspoon salt

Container capacity: 1¼ cups (300 ml)
Pickling time: 1 hour
Lifespan: 1 week refrigerated

1 Combine the sweet vinegar ingredients and mix well until the sugar and salt are dissolved. Cut the celery stalk into 6 inch (15 cm) lengths, then cut each piece into 3 to 4 strips. Use the leaves, too.
2 Pack the celery strips in a container, pour the sweet vinegar over and cover. Let stand at room temperature for 1 hour. Store in the refrigerator until serving.

Tomatoes Pickled in Sweet Vinegar

Pickling tomatoes makes them even more delicious and succulent. Here, the umami-rich juices from the tomatoes are enhanced by the sweet vinegar.

3 small tomatoes, about 5 oz (150 g) total

FOR THE SWEET VINEGAR
4 tablespoons rice vinegar
⅓ cup (80 ml) water
2 tablespoons sugar
1 heaping teaspoon salt

Container capacity: 3⅓ cups (800 ml)
Pickling time: 90 minutes
Lifespan: 3 days refrigerated

1 Combine the sweet vinegar ingredients and mix well until the sugar and salt are dissolved. Cut the tomatoes into ¼ inch (6 mm) slices and layer in a container. Spoon the sweet vinegar over the tomatoes a little at a time.
2 Let stand for about 30 minutes. When the container becomes filled with the juice from the tomatoes, cover with a lid and refrigerate for another hour. Keep refrigerated until serving.

Eggplant in Sweet Mustard

The eggplants are firmly rubbed with salt, then wrung out to remove bitterness. The sweetened mustard sauce makes for a mouthwatering pickle!

3 small Asian eggplants, about 8 oz (240 g) total
1 scant teaspoon salt (2% of the weight of the eggplants)
2 tablespoons mirin
1 teaspoon karashi mustard powder
5 teaspoons sugar

Container capacity: 4 cups (1 liter)
Pickling time: 8 hours
Lifespan: 5 days refrigerated

1 Remove the calyxes from the eggplants and cut in half lengthwise, then slice thinly crosswise. Transfer the eggplant slices to a bowl, sprinkle with salt and rub the salt in firmly.

2 When the eggplant starts to exude brown liquid, squeeze it tightly to wring out as much moisture as possible. Discard this liquid, which contains much of the bitterness.

3 Arrange the eggplant in a container. Mix the mirin and mustard powder together and pour over the eggplant. Sprinkle the sugar over.

4 Press the seasonings from step 3 into the eggplant with your fingertips. Cover and let stand for 8 hours. Store in the refrigerator until serving.

Mizuna Greens in Mustard Soy Sauce

Crisp mizuna greens are wilted with salt and seasoned with mustard and light soy sauce. You can also use mustard greens. A great change-of-pace side dish.

7 oz (200 g) mizuna greens
⅔ teaspoon salt (2% of the weight
of the mizuna)
½ teaspoon karashi mustard
powder
½ tablespoon light (usukuchi) soy
sauce

Container capacity: 8½ cups (2 liters)
Pickling time: 30 minutes
Lifespan: 3 days refrigerated

1 Cut the greens into 1 inch (2.5 cm) pieces. Place in a bowl and sprinkle with the salt. Set a 2 pound (1 kg) weight on top for 30 minutes. Remove the weight and squeeze the greens to remove liquid.
2 Mix the mustard powder into the soy sauce and pour over the mizuna greens. Massage well to coat. Let stand for 30 minutes at room temperature. Store in the refrigerator until serving.

Daikon in Mustard Soy Sauce

Mustard becomes mild and flavorful instead of strong and pungent when it's combined with the daikon radish. Make sure to squeeze out all excess moisture from the daikon radish to preserve its crunchy texture.

Piece daikon radish, about 10 oz (300 g)
1 teaspoon salt (2% of the weight
of the radish)
½ teaspoon karashi mustard powder
½ tablespoon light (usukuchi) soy sauce

Container capacity: 8½ cups (2 liters)
Pickling time: 20 minutes
Lifespan: 5 days refrigerated

1 Peel the daikon radish, cut into quarters lengthwise and slice thinly crosswise. Place in a bowl, sprinkle the salt over and rub in well. Place a 2 pound (1 kg) weight on top for one hour.
2 Squeeze the daikon radish well to remove all moisture. Mix the mustard powder and the soy sauce together and pour over the daikon radish. Massage well to coat. Let stand at room temperature for 20 minutes. Store in the refrigerator until serving.

Daikon, Cucumber and Carrot in Sweet Koji

Rice koji is steamed rice that has been inoculated with the *Aspergillus oryzae* mold. It's used to make all kinds of fermented foods in Japan. Pickles made with rice koji are mild and tasty.

Piece daikon radish, about 7 oz (200 g)
½ carrot, about 3½ oz (100 g)
2 small cucumbers or 1 large cucumber, about 7 oz (200 g) total
2 teaspoons salt (2% of the total weight of the vegetables), plus 1 additional teaspoon
3½ oz (100 g) Sweet Rice Koji (recipe below)

Container capacity: 4 cups (1 liter)
Pickling time: 8 hours
Lifespan: 3 days in the refrigerator

1 Peel the daikon and carrot, cut into quarters lengthwise and slice thinly. Slice the cucumber into thin diagonal slices (discard seeds if they are large). Put the vegetables in a bowl, sprinkle with 2 teaspoons of salt and leave for 1 hour. Squeeze out the excess moisture.

2 Add the additional 1 teaspoon salt to the Sweet Rice Koji and mix into the vegetables.

3 Set a 3½ pound (1.5 kg) weight on the vegetables and let stand for 8 hours at room temperature. Store in the refrigerator until serving.

Sweet Rice Koji

9 oz (250 g) dry rice koji
1⅔ cups (400 ml) water

Break up any lumps in the rice koji. Place in the bowl of a rice cooker, add the water and switch to the "Keep Warm" setting. After 2 hours, the rice koji will have fermented and have a porridge-like texture. Let cool, then refrigerate. Instead of rice cooker, you can use a yogurt maker or thermos. You'll need a food thermometer. Put the rice and water in a pan and heat on low until it reaches between 131 to 140°F (55 to 60°C). Put the mixture in the yogurt maker or thermos and let rest for 2 hours. Check to see if it has a porridge-like consistency. If not, leave up to 4 more hours.

Soybeans Pickled in Soy Sauce Koji

This rice-koji pickling bed is made with soy sauce for a deep, rich flavor. The fermented rice koji adds a subtle sweetness to the pickled beans. These are very useful to have on hand to accompany drinks or add to side dishes.

⅓ cup (50 g) boiled soybeans
7 oz (200 g) Soy Sauce Koji (recipe below)

Container capacity: 2 cups (500 ml)
Pickling time: 8 hours
Lifespan: 2 weeks refrigerated

1 Combine the Soy Sauce Koji and cooked soybeans in a container.

2 Stir well so that the soybeans are fully coated with the Soy Sauce Koji.

3 Cover and let stand for 8 hours. When the flavor has penetrated the soybeans, they are ready. Refrigerate until serving.

Soy Sauce Koji

3½ oz (100 g) dry rice koji
7 tablespoons soy sauce

Break up any lumps in the rice koji. Put the rice koji in a container and pour the soy sauce over it. Mix well, cover and leave at room temperature for 3 to 5 days to ferment, stirring once or twice a day. When the rice koji grains are soft, not chewy, the Soy Sauce Koji is ready. Store in the refrigerator. Yields 7 oz (200 g), for use in the recipe above.

More Reasons to Enjoy Pickles

Quick pickles are better than salad!

Admittedly, quick pickles do not have the same depth of flavor as vegetables pickled in the traditional way, with long fermentation. Even if they are only pickled for a short period, however, they still have that great fermented flavor that makes them far tastier than plain raw vegetables. In addition, they still retain the crunch and texture of raw vegetables. Furthermore, since vegetables for quick pickles are cut thinly or briefly parboiled to help seasonings penetrate quickly, they need only a little salt, so they have a light, refreshing flavor.

Quick pickling also reduces the volume of the vegetables. This means it's easy to eat a lot of them, which is a great way to add nutrients to your diet . They are also low in calories, since they don't need oily dressings to make them taste good.

Making a salad ahead of time can be a challenge as vegetables wilt and become soft, but quick-pickled vegetables will keep for at least two to three days, making planning and meal prep far easier. Another positive feature of quick pickles is that you can make them at any time. This means you can pickle ingredients or vegetables you need to use up in your refrigerator and season them with what you have in your pantry.

Pickles are seasoning, too

Salty, tangy and umami-filled, pickles are brimming with flavor! This means they can be added to bring another seasoning dimension to main dishes. They contain all the nutrients and texture of vegetables, too, so you can use them to vary many kinds of dishes quickly and easily. For instance, rice-bran pickles will add character and fragrance to any mixed-vegetable side dish. Umeboshi will add a touch of piquancy to fish dishes, and will counteract any fishy odors when added to the simmering liquid. Pickled wild vegetables and aromatic herbs can be chopped up and used to make appetizing dipping sauces. Try chopping up pickles and cooking them with steamed rice, or adding them to fried rice. Combining pickles with rice and other ingredients will expand your cooking repertoire immensely.

CHAPTER 2

Classic Pickles

In this chapter you'll find recipes for the pickles that are standard mealtime fare throughout Japan. They include rice-bran pickles, umeboshi (salt-preserved ume fruit), salt-pickled napa cabbage, and pickles made with sake lees. It may seem a little daunting at first to tackle them, but once you've tried making your own you'll find that it's surprisingly easy. I hope you'll also enjoy trying the alternatives to traditional methods I've come up with over many years, such as wheat-bran pickles (see page 39) and my recipe Sa Shi Su Umeboshi—a foolproof way of making the iconic pickled plum. And remember, pickles aren't just for eating as a side dish—I also recommend using them as seasonings in main dishes. In this chapter, as well as recipes for traditional pickles, you'll also find a selection of recipes for main dishes that incorporate your homemade pickles as seasonings, imparting an unbeatable flavor and fragrance.

Rice Bran Pickles

In Japanese, "nuka" refers to rice bran, the coarse outer layers of rice grains that are removed when rice is milled. Nukazuke—vegetables pickled in a well-fermented bed of rice bran—have a mouthwatering tang and aroma. This is one of the definitive pickle types in Japanese cuisine, and here I'll show you how to make your own rice-bran bed for pickling. If you start the bed in the spring, by summer the lactic acid bacteria will be multiplying rapidly, allowing you use the bed to make tasty pickles well into the fall. I'll start with the basic pickling bed (facing page), then I'll explain "throw-away" pickling and the main pickling process (page 38).

2 lbs (1 kg) fresh rice bran
5 oz (150 g) salt
2 tablespoons dry-roasted soybeans (or regular dried soybeans, roasted in a skillet over low heat until lightly browned)
One 2 x 6 in (5 x 15 cm) piece dry kombu seaweed
3 small dried red chili peppers
3⅓ cups (800 ml) water

Container capacity: 17 cups (4 liters)
Pickling time: Several hours
Lifespan: 1 to 2 days

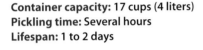

MAKING THE RICE BRAN PICKLING BED

A rice-bran pickling bed or base (*nukadoko*) is made from rice bran, salt and water. Adding aromatic ingredients helps encourage fermentation and good flavor. Use a lidded container, keep in a cool place and mix it up well every day.

1 Measure the rice bran in a large bowl. Add the salt in several batches, mixing well with each addition.

2 Add the water a little at a time, mixing it in with your hands so it is absorbed.

3 Keep squeezing the mixture with your hands to ensure that the moisture is evenly distributed.

4 Knead the rice bran with both hands. It should be soft enough to squeeze easily through your fingers. (If using roasted rice bran, you may need a little more water than called for in the recipe.) The mixture should be moist, but not soggy.

5 Transfer the rice-bran bed to a nonreactive container a little at a time. Press down well after each addition to eliminate any air pockets.

6 Add the dry-roasted soybeans, kombu seaweed and red chili peppers, burying them in the rice bran bed for added flavor.

PRELIMINARY OR "THROW-AWAY" PICKLING

In the next stage of making a rice-bran pickling bed, vegetable scraps are added and discarded once a day for three or four days running. This helps the pickling bed to ferment and gives it a well-rounded flavor that produces delicious pickles. Use about a quarter of the total weight of the rice-bran pickling bed. For example, use 8 ounces (250 g) of vegetables for every 2 pounds (1 kg) of base.

1 Make a well in the middle of the pickling bed and add some vegetable scraps. Possibilities include the outer leaves of a cabbage, radish or turnip tops, the tail ends of a daikon radish, and so on.

2 Cover the vegetable scraps with the rice-bran bed, smooth out the surface and cover the container with a lid. Leave the bed for 12 to 24 hours, then remove and discard the vegetable scraps. Do this for three to four days in a row. Taste a bit of one of the scraps as you remove it. If it's tangy and flavorful, the pickling bed is ready.

MAKING THE PICKLES

At last, it's time to make rice-bran pickles. Try not to put too many vegetables in the bed. Ideally you'll want to just pickle the quantity that you and your family can eat in a day, every day. This is a delicious way to benefit from the vitamins in the vegetables, and the lactic acid and nutrients from the rice bran.

This is just an example of the vegetables you can pickle in your rice-bran pickling bed. The amounts given are appropriate for the pickling bed recipe outlined above.

1 large or 2 small cucumbers
2 small Asian eggplants or 1 large eggplant
½ medium carrot

Tip: Incorporate flavor-improving vegetables as you go! Try adding aromatic ingredients such as garlic cloves or dried orange peel to your bed as you use it. This will give your pickles even more complexity and interest.

1 Small Asian eggplants may be added whole. Large eggplants should be cut lengthwise into halves or quarters. Cut the cucumbers and carrot into halves or quarters lengthwise, too, depending on how big they are. For the first few times you use a newly made pickling bed, you will not need salt, since the bed itself will be quite salty. After that, rub a small amount of salt into the surface of the vegetables before pickling.

2 Push the vegetables firmly into the pickling bed. Cover with pickling bed so that they are completely buried.

3 Smooth out the surface and cover with a lid. Leave to ferment at room temperature for 5 to 7 hours. Just before serving, take the vegetables out, briefly rinse off the rice bran and cut them up into bite-sized pieces.

All About Rice Bran Pickling

In Japan it's fairly easy to obtain fresh rice bran from supermarkets and stores where rice is milled, but if you can't find it where you live, there are a couple of substitutes you can use.

The best substitute is dry-roasted rice bran (*irinuka*), available online and from well-stocked Japanese grocery stores. This is rice bran that has been slowly roasted until the moisture has mostly evaporated. It keeps much better than fresh or raw rice bran, but the roasting kills most of the microbes in the bran. Still, you can make a pickle bed with this as the base. Simply use the same quantity of dry-roasted rice bran as the fresh rice bran called for in the recipe and add a little more water than called for so the pickling bed is the right consistency. Be sure to get plain rice bran with no added seasonings.

Another substitute, if you have access to a mill, is fresh wheat bran. Make sure it is free of any impurities before you use it. The pickles may taste different from those produced with rice bran, but they will still be good. All types of bran should be stored in a cool, dark place and be used up quickly, or they may turn rancid. Fresh bran can be frozen for up to a month.

Q1 How should I maintain my rice-bran pickling bed?

A Stir up the bed completely twice a day, morning and evening, even if you don't make pickles. This adjusts the amount of bacteria in the pickling bed to keep it at an optimum level. Once a day is the bare minimum. If you just let it sit, your pickles will taste bad.

Q2 What should I do if the pickling bed becomes watery?

A If moisture from the vegetables makes the pickling bed too wet, add more rice bran and knead it in well. Alternatively, wrap some dried daikon radish strips (*kiriboshi daikon*, available at Japanese grocery stores) in cheesecloth and bury them in the bed. You can eat the daikon afterward, too!

Q3 Should I remove the white mold-like growth on the surface of the pickling bed?

A The thin white growth you may see on the surface of your pickling bed is not a bad mold; it's a type of yeast similar to the one formed in wine-making. You can simply stir it back into the pickling bed, or scoop it off with a spoon and discard. But black or pink-red mold is dangerous. If either of these begins to form, discard the pickling bed and start a new one.

Q4 What should I do when I'm away or can't attend to the pickling bed for an extended period?

A If you can't attend to your pickling bed for up to a week, just put it in the fridge. You can also transfer the pickling bed to well-sealed plastic bags to store. If you'll be away for a longer time, the pickling bed can be frozen; to use it again, let it defrost at room temperature. If the weather is hot and humid, the bed may ferment too fast and turn sour. If this happens, refrigerate it for a while to let it recover.

Rice Bran Pickles in a Bag

For this method, the vegetables are pickled briefly in salt. Then a porous bag of rice bran is placed on top to transfer the flavor and goodness of the bran to the pickles. This is an easy way to enjoy rice-bran pickles without having to make a pickling bed. See the facing page for how to make a rice-bran bag.

Rice Bran Pickled Cabbage

1½ lbs (700 g) cabbage
½ oz (14 g) salt (2% of the weight of the cabbage)
3½ oz (100 g) fresh or dry-roasted rice bran

Container capacity: 12 cups (3 liters)
Pickling time: A few hours
Lifespan: 2 to 3 days

1 Cut the cabbage into bite-sized pieces and place in a large bowl. Add the salt and rub it into the cabbage well.

2 Set a 5½ pound (2.5 kg) weight on top of the cabbage (you may need to put a small plate on top of the cabbage first to make the pressure even). Let stand for 30 minutes to an hour.

3 Check to see if the cabbage has started to give off moisture. If not, leave the weight on for a little while longer.

4 Wet the rice-bran bag (below) and wring out well. Fill with the rice bran. Fold the flap inside to keep the bran from spilling out.

5 Place the rice-bran bag on top of the cabbage, arranging it in the bowl so that it covers the cabbage.

6 Set a 5½ pound (2.5 kg) weight on top of the rice-bran bag. Let stand for 6 hours. Refrigerate until serving.

Frequently Asked Questions

Q1 How is the rice-bran bag made?

A Fold a 2 foot (60 cm) long piece of cheesecloth or unbleached muslin in two, with one part 3 inches (8 cm) longer than the other half. Sew up the sides, leaving the part with the overlap unsewn. If you'd rather avoid sewing, you can wrap the rice bran in a flat piece of cheesecloth like a parcel instead.

Q2 How often can I use the rice-bran bag?

A The bag can essentially be used indefinitely. The more you use it, the more moisture, salt and flavor it will absorb from the vegetables. When the liquid that comes out of it starts to get cloudy and the flavor becomes flat, add more rice bran to the bag.

Rice Bran Sprinkling Method

With this easy pickling method, the vegetables are first sprinkled with salt, then with rice bran, and are ready in about half a day. No pickling bed is required. The pickles have a wonderfully crunchy texture.

Rice Bran Pickle Showcase
Here's a colorful arrangement of rice-bran pickles, including turnip, turnip greens, apples, celery and radish. Any of the three rice-bran pickling methods described— the traditional pickling bed (page 37), the bag method (page 40), or the sprinkle-on method (page 42)—can be used to pickle these ingredients. No matter how you do it, they'll all be delicious.

Rice Bran Pickled Daikon Radish

1 daikon radish, about 1¾ lbs (800 g), 1 foot (30 cm) long
1 medium apple
3½ oz (100 g) fresh rice bran or dry-roasted rice bran (more as needed)
3 small dried red chili peppers
2 heaping tablespoons salt

Container capacity: 8½ cups (2 liters)
Pickling time: A few hours
Lifespan: 2–3 days

1 Peel the daikon and cut lengthwise into 4 pieces. Cut the apple in half vertically and slice thinly. Sprinkle a thin layer of the rice bran on the bottom of the container and arrange the daikon radish pieces over it.

2 Add the chili peppers and sprinkle the salt evenly over all.

3 Distribute the apple slices on top of the salted daikon radish.

4 Sprinkle in enough rice bran to cover the apple completely.

5 Place a plate or board on top of the rice bran, then place a 6½ pound (3 kg) weight on top of the rice bran. When the rice bran has become moist, reduce the weight by half. Leave at room temperature for 6 to 8 hours. When the daikon radish has taken on the flavor of the rice bran, the pickles are ready. The apple can be eaten, too, if you wish.

Scallops with Rice Bran Pickles

The fragrance and subtle saltiness of rice-bran pickles are used here to flavor sashimi. Use whatever pickled vegetables you like, thinly sliced or finely minced.

Serves 2

6 large, fresh, sushi-grade scallops
2 radishes pickled in rice bran (see page 42)
1 tablespoon each finely minced rice-bran-pickled
cucumber, daikon radish and apple (page 42)

1 Slice the scallops thinly.
2 Slice the radish pickles thinly. Finely mince the leaves.
3 Combine the scallops with all the pickled vegetables. Toss gently so that the flavors mingle.

Stir-fried Pork and Pickled Cabbage

When pickles are stir-fried, their taste and texture become even more delicious, thanks to the addition of oil and the evaporation of moisture. Pickled cabbage goes very well with pork, making this a great main dish for dinner.

Serves 2

3½ oz (100 g) thinly sliced pork shoulder
7 oz (200 g) Rice-bran-pickled Cabbage (page 40)
1 tablespoon rapeseed or canola oil
Coarsely ground black pepper to taste

1 Cut the pork into bite-sized pieces. Squeeze out the excess moisture from the pickled cabbage.
2 Heat the oil in a skillet. Add the pork and stir-fry until it changes color. Add the pickled cabbage and stir-fry until cabbage softens. Add black pepper just before serving.

Pickled Daikon Radish and Salmon Rolls

Using the salt from the pickles to marinate the salmon eliminates the need for the soy sauce that is usually served with sushi. Crunchy daikon radish and tender salmon make a great combination.

Serves 2

1 piece Rice-bran-pickled Daikon Radish (page 42)
5 oz (150 g) fresh sushi-grade salmon, cut for use as sashimi or sushi
3 in (7 cm) green onion, cut into thin ribbons

1 Slice the pickled daikon thinly lengthwise into wide ribbons. Cut the salmon in half lengthwise.
2 Place three or four slices of the daikon radish pickle on a sushi roll mat lengthwise. Put a piece of salmon across the near edge of the ribbons and roll up. Repeat to make two rolls.
3 Slice the rolls into ¾ inch (2 cm) wide pieces. Serve with the green onion on the side.

Umeboshi Pickled Plums

Umeboshi are the preserved fruit of the ume tree, a type of apricot (though they are often called plums). They keep very well, and can be used for cooking or simply eaten as is. They have numerous health benefits in addition to being delicious. If you've never tried to make your own umeboshi, please try my easy Sa Shi Su Umeboshi first (see facing page). The ume vinegar that is a by-product of making umeboshi will add extra sparkle to anything you cook.

Sa Shi Su Umeboshi

"Sa" is for *sato*, or sugar; "shi" is for *shio*, salt; and *su* means vinegar. This is an easy version of umeboshi that is made by simply adding sugar, salt and vinegar to the fruit. Since the ume fruit are not preserved in salt, there is no danger of them becoming moldy. The pickling liquid is delicious, too!

2 lbs (1 kg) ripe ume fruit, rinsed and patted dry
1½ cups (300 g) sugar
3½ oz (100 g) salt
3⅓ cups (800 ml) rice vinegar, plus more for cleaning the jar

Container capacity: 10 to 12 cups (2.5 to 3 liters)
Pickling time: 2 weeks or more
Lifespan: 6 months without drying;
**   1 to 2 years if dried (see page 48)**

1 Wash and dry the jar well. Moisten a clean paper towel with extra vinegar and wipe the inside of the jar. Remove the stem end of each ume fruit with a skewer or toothpick. Place the fruit in a jar.

2 Add the salt and sugar.

3 Swirl in the vinegar. Push the salt and sugar in between the ume so that it sinks to the bottom of the jar.

4 Cover the jar and leave in a cool, dark place for at least two weeks, or until good drying weather is predicted (see page 48). Shake the jar occasionally to help the salt and sugar dissolve.

Drying Ume Fruit

Drying out the ume fruit after the initial pickling will greatly improve the texture and flavor. This is usually done during the hottest days of the summer. The 18-day period before the first day of autumn, called *doyo* in Japanese, is usually the best time to do this, so the process is commonly called "doyo drying." Umeboshi made with the Sa Shi Su method benefit greatly from this drying step, and it's also an essential part of making traditional Red Shiso Umeboshi (see page 50).

1 When the weather forecast predicts several days of hot, sunny weather (late July or early August in the northern hemisphere), use a wooden spoon to gently transfer the ume from the pickling liquid to a colander or sieve. Drain, being careful not to break the fruit. Reserve the pickling liquid separately to use as seasoning.

2 Spread the ume out on a flat sieve or rack. Leave them to dry outside for three days and nights, turning once a day. Take them in if rain threatens, adding additional drying time to make up for the rainy spell. After three full days and nights of drying, transfer the umeboshi to a storage container. Keep in a cool, dark place until use.

Sa Shi Su Small Umeboshi

Small ume fruit can be pickled using the Sa Shi Su method. These small umeboshi are particularly nice to have on hand for making bento-box lunches and serving with green tea. They also add a piquant note to meals at the table.

1 lb (500 g) ripe small ume fruit
¾ cup (150 g) sugar
1⅓ oz (50 g) salt
1⅔ cups (400 ml) rice vinegar
Extra vinegar to clean the jar

Container capacity: 6½ to 8½ cups (1.5 to 2 liters)
Pickling time: 2 weeks or more
Lifespan: 6 months without drying; 1 to 2 years if dried

1 Rinse the small ume fruit carefully under running water and transfer to a colander or sieve to drain. Meanwhile, wash and dry the jar and wipe the inside with a vinegar-moistened paper towel.

2 Pat the ume fruit dry gently. You don't have to remove the stem ends as you would with larger fruit.

3 Carefully place the ume fruit in a jar and add the salt and sugar.

4 Pour the vinegar over the fruit and cover the jar with a lid. Leave in a cool, dark place for two weeks or more. If desired, dry for three days and nights as directed on page 48. These pickled ume may be eaten without drying.

Red Shiso Umeboshi

These tart-and-salty red umeboshi are the classic old-fashioned type. The ume fruit are first salted, then dyed with the red shiso leaves and finally dried. Keep the finished umeboshi in a tightly covered jar or crock in a cool place; they will continue to mature.

2 lbs (1 kg) ripe ume fruit
5 oz (150 g) salt
3½ oz (100 g) fresh red shiso leaves

Container capacity: 6½ to 8½ cups (1.5 to 2 liters)
Pickling time: 2 weeks or more
Lifespan: 2 to 3 years

1 Soak the ume fruit in water for 6 hours to remove bitterness. Drain, then dry each fruit gently with a paper towel. Carefully remove the stem ends with a wooden skewer or toothpick. Roll each fruit in the salt and place it in the container. Layer the salted fruit; the upper layers should have more salt than the lower layers. Add any remaining salt to the container.

2 Place a small plate that fits into the container directly on top of the fruit, and set a 6½ lb (3 kg) weight on the plate. Cover the jar and let stand for about a week, until the liquid released by the fruit reaches the top level of the fruit. Drain the fruit, reserving ⅔ cup (150 ml) of the liquid (known as "white ume vinegar" for step 4 of this recipe. (You can keep any extra white ume vinegar for use in other recipes and as seasoning.)

3 Wash the red shiso leaves well and pat dry. Place in a bowl and add ⅓ cup (75 ml) of the reserved white ume vinegar from step 2. Squeeze firmly several times.

4 When dark purple liquid starts coming out of the leaves, wring them out well and discard the liquid. Add the remaining ⅓ cup (75 ml) of white ume vinegar. Squeeze the leaves firmly again several times, then wring out the liquid and discard.

5 Line the bottom of a jar with a third of the wrung-out red shiso leaves. Arrange the fruit in the jar, then top with the remaining leaves. Set a 1 pound (500 g) weight on top, then cover the container and leave in a cool, dark place until several days of hot, sunny weather are forecast.

6 Spread the fruit and leaves on a flat sieve or a rack. Dry for three days and nights as directed on page 48. Pack the dried fruit into a crock or jar, cover tightly, and keep in a cool, dark place until use.

Frequently Asked Questions

Q1 Is it possible to reduce the amount of salt when making Red Shiso Umeboshi?

A If you reduce the amount of salt used in the first stage of pickling, you risk the ume getting moldy. The minimum amount of salt is 13 percent of the weight of the fruit; 15 percent is best. Small ume fruit can be pickled with 10 percent of their weight in salt, but it is important to watch carefully for mold in that case.

Q2 I tried salting my ume and they turned moldy! How can I prevent this?

A If the amount of salt is insufficient, or if the container is left in a humid location, mold may grow. If there are only a few fruit with tiny specks of mold, they can be scooped out. You can also try spraying the ume first with shochu or other high-alcohol distilled liquor, like vodka.

Q3 Can I make classic umeboshi without red shiso leaves?

A Umeboshi are delicious even without the red shiso leaves. Follow the steps 1 and 2 on page 50, then proceed directly with sun-drying. Undyed umeboshi take on a subtle red hue when they are dried.

Q4 Will Sa Shi Su Umeboshi mature and improve in flavor like classic umeboshi?

A Umeboshi made with the Sa Shi Su method become sweeter when they are dried. If the umeboshi are stored separately from the pickling liquid, their flavor will mellow, but they will still be delicious.

Q5 Can I skip the drying step for Sa Shi Su Umeboshi ?

A One of the benefits of the Sa Shi Su method is that the ume pickled in sweet-sour vinegar can be eaten as is, without drying. They will be juicier than dried umeboshi, but they must be consumed within a few months or they will get mushy and fall apart. If you want to keep the umeboshi for a long time, it is better to dry them.

Frozen Ume in Sugar

If you happen to have leftover fresh ume fruit, freeze some to make this delicious dessert or snack. When sugar is added to the frozen fruit, they exude a large amount of delicious ume syrup.

1 lb (500 g) ripe ume fruit
¾ cup (150 g) sugar (30% of the weight of the ume fruit)

Container capacity: 4 cups (1 liter)
Pickling time: 12 to 13 days
Lifespan: 3 months at room temperature

1 Wash the ume fruit, pat dry and remove the stem ends with a wooden skewer or toothpick. Pack into a 1-quart (1 liter) freezer bag and freeze. To begin making the dessert, arrange the frozen ume fruit and sugar in a jar in alternating layers.

2 Cover the jar tightly and leave at room temperature. After two to three days the sugar will start to dissolve; shake the jar every so often to hasten the process. The fruit will be ready after 12 days or so. Serve the sweet ume as a snack or light dessert. The syrup can be mixed with soda water for a refreshing drink.

Frozen Ume Preserved in Miso

Frozen ume is mixed with miso and allowed to defrost. As the ume juice melts into the miso, a perfectly balanced blend of umami and tartness is created. Eat as is or use in various recipes as a seasoning.

1 lb (500 g) ripe ume fruit
1 lb (500 g) miso paste
1½ cups (300 g) sugar

Container capacity: 6½ to 8 ½ cups (1.5 to 2 liters)
Pickling time: 2½ to 3 weeks
Lifespan: 3 months at room temperature

1 Wash the ume fruit, pat dry and remove the stem ends with a bamboo skewer. Pack into 1-quart (1 liter) freezer bag and freeze. When you are ready to begin making the pickles, combine the miso with the sugar and mix well.

2 Spread a thin layer of the miso-sugar paste on the bottom of the container.

3 Arrange the frozen ume fruit and the remaining miso-sugar paste in alternating layers in the container. Cover the top layer of the ume fruit with the last of the miso-sugar paste. Cover tightly and leave at room temperature for about a week, until the miso and the juice from the fruit have started to mingle. After about 10 more days, the preserve will be ready. The sweet miso sauce may be used in cooking.

Sa Shi Su Pickled Apricots

Apricots, which are far less tart than ume fruit, can be pickled with a small amount of "Sa Shi Su" pickling liquid and stored without drying. Apricots pickled in this way are a real pick-me-up!

2 lbs (1 kg) ripe apricots
1 oz (30 g) salt
⅔ cup (130 g) sugar
7 tablespoons vinegar

Container capacity: 8½ cups (2 liters)
Pickling time: 1 month
Lifespan: 6 months in a cool dark
place

1 Wash the apricots and pat dry. Transfer to a large bowl and sprinkle with the salt. Mix to distribute the salt evenly, then split each apricot in half with your hands. Do not remove the pits.

2 Place a small plate directly on the fruit and set a 2 pound (1 kg) weight on top. Leave for 8 hours, until plenty of liquid has come out of the fruit.

3 Arrange the apricots and sugar in alternating layers in a jar. Pour the vinegar over. Cover tightly and allow to pickle in a cool, dark place for one month. Consume within six months.

Sa Shi Su Umeboshi Rice

The rice is cooked with the umeboshi, pits and all, so that it takes up as much as the piquant flavor as possible. It's terrific in bento-box lunches.

Serves 2 to 4

1½ cups (300 g) uncooked Japanese rice

¾ cup (200 ml) water, plus more for soaking

6 Sa Shi Su Umeboshi (page 47)

1 Rinse the rice. Soak in water to cover for 30 minutes. Drain and transfer to a rice cooker. Add the ¾ cup of water and Sa Shi Su Umeboshi. Cook on the regular setting. If you don't have a rice cooker, soak and drain the rice, and put in a heavy pan with a tight fitting lid with the ¾ cup of water and Sa Shi Su Umeboshi. Bring to a boil, then put on the lid. Lower the heat to the lowest setting. Cook for 13 minutes. Turn off the heat, and leave to rest, lid on, for 10 minutes.
2 When the rice is cooked, mix it, crushing the umeboshi until they are distributed evenly. Remove pits and serve.

Sa Shi Su Yakisoba Noodles

The only seasoning in this dish is the pickling vinegar from Sa Shi Su Umeboshi. It adds a tangy goodness to the noodles, vegetables and meat that will leave you wanting more. This recipe also works well with cooked spaghettini or spaghetti instead of yakisoba.

Serves 2

1 large cabbage leaf
1 green onion
2 fresh shiitake mushrooms
2 portions ready-made soft yakisoba noodles (available at Japanese grocery stores)
1 tablespoon rapeseed or canola oil
3½ oz (100 g) thinly sliced beef
3 tablespoons Sa Shi Su Umeboshi pickling vinegar (page 47)

1 Chop the cabbage roughly. Thinly slice the green onion diagonally. Remove the stems from the shiitake mushrooms and slice into thin strips.
2 Put the yakisoba noodles in a skillet and add a little water to separate them. Stir-fry for a couple of minutes, then remove from the pan.
3 Heat the oil in the skillet. Add the beef, then add the vegetables and stir-fry until cabbage is tender.
4 Return the noodles to the pan and stir-fry until heated through. Swirl in the Sa Shi Su Umeboshi pickling vinegar to season.

Sa Shi Su Soy-milk Cottage Cheese

Mix Sa Shi Su pickling vinegar with soy milk to make instant cottage cheese with a mild flavor. You can use a coffee filter to strain the curds instead of paper towels.

Serves 2 to 4

1⅔ cups (400 ml) unsweetened soy milk
2 tablespoons Sa Shi Su Umeboshi pickling vinegar (page 47)
Bread of your choice

1 Heat the soy milk in a pan until it bubbles gently. Remove from the heat and stir in the pickling vinegar.
2 Continue stirring until the curds start to separate from the whey. Set a paper-towel-lined colander over a bowl and strain the soy-milk mixture to remove the whey. Transfer the curds to a serving dish. Serve alongside the bread.

Simmered Sardines with Small Umeboshi

The tang of the umeboshi brings out the umami of the sardines. The simmering liquid is reduced to make a sweet sauce.

Serves 2

2 large fresh sardines
3 tablespoons mirin
1 tablespoon soy sauce
7 tablespoons water
2 Sa Shi Su Small Umeboshi (page 49)

1 Cut the heads off the sardines and remove the intestines. Rinse quickly under cold running water and pat dry.
2 Bring the mirin, soy sauce and water to a boil in a saucepan. Add the cleaned sardines and small umeboshi. Simmer, uncovered, for about 6 minutes.
3 When the sardines are cooked through and the liquid in the pan is reduced by about a half, turn off the heat. Serve with the small umeboshi.

Daikon with Red Shiso Umeboshi

The sourness of the umeboshi makes a perfect foil for the daikon radish. The daikon radish is wilted with salt first, and the red shiso leaves are a colorful accent.

Serves 2

Piece daikon radish, about 3½ oz (100 g)
1 Red Shiso Umeboshi (page 50)
⅓ teaspoon salt (2% of the weight of the daikon radish)
A few red shiso leaves from Red Shiso Umeboshi

1 Cut the daikon radish into very thin 1½ inch (4 cm) long strips. Sprinkle with the salt and let stand for about 20 minutes. Squeeze out any excess moisture.
2 Pit the umeboshi, reserving the pit. Place the umeboshi flesh and pit and the daikon radish strips in a bowl. Stir to combine. Remove the pit and arrange the daikon radish on a serving dish. Garnish with the red shiso leaves.

Sautéed Chicken with Sa Shi Su Pickled Apricots

The fruity pickled apricots are great with chicken. The pickling vinegar tenderizes the chicken and makes it very juicy.

Serves 2

2 boneless chicken thighs, about 6 oz (170 g) total
3 tablespoons pickling vinegar from Sa Shi Su Pickled Apricots (page 54)
½ small turnip
2 Sa Shi Su Pickled Apricots
Rapeseed or canola oil for sautéing

1 Cut the chicken into bite-sized pieces. Sprinkle with the pickling vinegar and let stand for 5 minutes. Cut the turnip in half, then cut into ⅓ inch (1 cm) thick slices.
2 Heat the oil in a skillet. Add the chicken pieces, skin-side down. When browned, turn over, add the turnip and sauté.
3 Arrange on plates with the pickled apricots.

Cold Tofu with Frozen Ume Miso

The rich sauce that is produced by the Frozen Ume Preserved in Miso recipe is great on tofu or vegetables. The sauce can be used to season a wide variety of dishes.

Serves 2

½ block firm tofu, about 3½ oz (100 g)
1 tablespoon sauce from Frozen Ume Preserved in Miso (page 53)
Thinly sliced green onion, for garnish

1 Quarter the tofu and arrange on two plates.
2 Spoon the miso sauce from Frozen Ume Preserved in Miso over the tofu. Garnish with the green onion. You can also try crushing one of the preserved ume and mixing it with the miso sauce.

Sugared Ume and Pomelo

Simply combine ume in sugar with citrus fruit to make an elegant dessert. Spoon the rich, sweet ume syrup over the fruit before serving.

Serves 2

½ pomelo or grapefruit
2 Frozen Ume in Sugar (page 52), plus syrup
A few mint leaves for garnish

1 Peel and segment the pomelo. Remove the membranes from each segment.
2 Divide the pomelo segments and frozen ume between two serving bowls. Spoon the syrup over the fruit. Garnish with mint leaves.

Pickled Napa Cabbage

Napa (Chinese) cabbage pickled in salt is a fixture on the Japanese dinner table in the cold months. The crisp chilled pickles are great with freshly cooked rice; they also make a nice drinking appetizer. This section includes a very easy cut-cabbage method as well as a kimchi-flavored version. Napa cabbage is wonderfully versatile!

Napa Cabbage Pickled in Salt

Choose very fresh napa cabbage and use the whole head. To make this simple pickle, each head is split into quarters, sprinkled with salt and flavored with kombu seaweed and red chili pepper. Once it's matured, store in the refrigerator.

2 large heads napa cabbage, 9 lbs (4 kg) total
2²⁄₃ oz (80 g) salt (2% of the weight of the cabbage)
Four 1½ inch (4 cm) square pieces kombu seaweed
3 small red chili peppers

Container capacity: 6¾ quarts (6 liters)
Pickling time: 3 days
Lifespan: 2 weeks at room temperature, plus 1 month refrigerated

1 Make a deep criss-cross cut into the root end of each cabbage. Starting from this cut, split the heads into quarters with your hands. Rub salt in between the leaves down to the root end. Sprinkle the rest of the salt evenly over the cabbages.

2 Layer the cabbage pieces in the container so that the root ends alternate with the leafy ends. Top each quarter with a piece of kombu and a chili pepper.

3 Press the cabbage down with your hands. Place a sturdy plate on top of the cabbage and press down again, using all your body weight.

4 Set a 26 pound (12 kg) weight on top of the plate. Let stand at room temperature for three days.

5 The pickled cabbage is ready to eat when a lot of liquid has come out. Store at room temperature for around 2 weeks. As soon as it begins to taste sour, transfer to the refrigerator and eat within a month.

Chopped Napa Cabbage Pickles

If you just need a small quantity of pickles, this method produces them overnight. Add some shredded kombu seaweed for umami and yuzu citrus for fragrance. This is an interesting change of pace from traditional napa cabbage pickles.

¼ head napa cabbage, about 1 lb (500 g)
2 teaspoons salt (2% of the weight of the cabbage)
⅓ oz (10 g) shredded kombu seaweed
2 red chili peppers
2 small ripe yellow yuzu citrus or Meyer lemons

Container capacity: 12 cups (3 liters)
Pickling time: 8 hours
Lifespan: 2 to 3 days refrigerated

1 Cut the leaf ends of the cabbage into 1 inch (2.5 cm) wide pieces. Cut the thicker stem parts a bit thinner, about ¾ inch (2 cm) wide. Cut the yuzu citrus into quarters.

2 In a large bowl, combine the napa cabbage with the salt, yuzu citrus and shredded kombu seaweed. Mix and squeeze well with your hands. Add the chili peppers.

3 Place a sturdy plate directly on the cabbage. Set a 3½ pound (1.5 kg) weight on the plate and leave for about 8 hours until a good amount of moisture has come out of the cabbage. Refrigerate until serving.

Napa Cabbage Kimchi

When your salt-pickled napa cabbage begins to turn sour, add some aromatic ingredients to create a spicy variation that takes its inspiration from Korean kimchi. The sesame oil and soy sauce add irresistibly fragrant goodness.

14 oz (400 g) Napa Cabbage Pickled in Salt (page 61)
3½ oz (100 g) flat garlic chives
2 tablespoons finely minced green onion
1 teaspoon grated garlic
2 anchovies
1 teaspoon red pepper powder*
2 teaspoons dark sesame oil
2 teaspoons light (usukuchi) soy sauce

* Use the type that is used for kimchi if possible. It's available at Korean grocery stores.

Container capacity: 10½ to 12 cups (2.5 to 3 liters)
Pickling time: 5 hours
Lifespan: A few days refrigerated

1 Cut the pickled napa cabbage into 1 inch (2.5 cm) wide pieces. Parboil the garlic chives for 2 minutes, then drain well and squeeze out the excess moisture. Cut into 1 inch (2.5 cm) pieces.

2 In a large bowl, combine the pickled cabbage, garlic chives, green onion, garlic, anchovies and ground red pepper. Mix well.

3 Toss and squeeze the vegetables with your hands so the seasonings coat them evenly. Let stand for 6 hours. Cover tightly and refrigerate until serving.

Pickled Napa Cabbage Sushi

The crispness and gentle savor of the pickled cabbage make these sushi rolls very easy to eat. They're filled with comforting Japanese omelet and spicy red pickled ginger, which contrasts well with the cabbage.

Serves 2

6 leaves Napa Cabbage Pickled in Salt (page 61)
1½ cups (300 g) cooked Japanese rice, still hot

FOR THE SUSHI VINEGAR
2 tablespoons rice vinegar
1½ teaspoons sugar
½ teaspoon salt

FOR THE OMELET
2 large eggs
2 teaspoons sugar
Pinch of salt
Rapeseed or canola oil for cooking
½ tablespoon beni-shoga pickled ginger (or use Young Ginger with Red Shiso, page 93)

1 Whisk together the sushi vinegar ingredients. Sprinkle over the hot cooked rice. Fold and mix the vinegar into the rice, taking care not to crush the grains. Allow to cool to room temperature.

2 Beat the eggs and whisk in the sugar and the salt. Heat the oil in a square tamagoyaki pan or a small skillet. Pour in a third of the egg mixture, cook until almost set on top and then roll it up to one end of the pan. Repeat with another third of the egg mixture, then the final third, adding to the roll each time. Remove the omelet from the pan and allow to cool, then cut in half lengthwise.

3 Lay three pickled cabbage leaves on a sushi rolling mat, alternating the leaf ends and stem ends. Spread out half of the seasoned rice onto the leaves.

4 Place one of the omelet halves across the center of the rice and top with pickled ginger, then roll up as for sushi. Repeat to make two rolls. Slice and arrange on a plate. If you like, serve with additional pickled ginger on the side.

Cabbage and Natto Pockets

This is a quick and easy dish. The pickled napa cabbage and natto (fermented soybeans) are stuffed into tofu-skin pouches, then cooked until golden brown. This is a great appetizer to serve with drinks.

Serves 2

4 tablespoons Chopped Napa Cabbage Pickles (page 62)
2 teaspoons natto
1 abura-age deep-fried tofu skin
¼ yuzu citrus, cut into 2 wedges

1 Cut the abura-age in half lengthwise and open up each half to make a pocket. Insert 2 tablespoons of the pickled cabbage and 1 teaspoon of the natto into each pocket. Secure the opening with a toothpick.
2 Heat a skillet and add the stuffed pockets (oil is not needed, as the tofu skins are deep-fried). Cook until browned on both sides.
3 Cut each pocket in half, leaving the toothpicks in place. Serve with a yuzu citrus wedge alongside.

Korean Tofu Stew

The pickled napa cabbage has far more umami than raw napa cabbage. The soy sauce adds even more savor to the flavorful soup. Cook this in an earthenware pot if possible.

Serves 2

7 oz (200 g) Napa Cabbage Kimchi (page 63)
Block soft tofu, about 7 oz (200 g)
1 green onion
1⅔ cups (400 ml) water
5–6 dried sardines (niboshi)
1 tablespoon light (usukuchi) soy sauce

1 Cut the tofu into 8 pieces. Thinly slice the green onion diagonally.
2 Bring the water and dried sardines to a boil in an earthenware or other heavy pot. Add the tofu, green onion and cabbage pickles. Simmer for 3 minutes. Remove from the heat and drizzle in the soy sauce to finish.

Pickled Onions

In Japan, pickled onions are often made with rakkyo (*Allium chinense*), also called Chinese onion. You may be able to find fresh rakkyo at well-stocked general Asian or Chinese grocery stores in the West. If not, try using small pickling onions, small shallots or bulbing scallions instead. Rakkyo are in season in early summer—put some up then, and you can keep eating them until the following year. Pickling with salt is the first step for making the standard sweet-vinegar-pickled rakkyo and the equally delicious soy-sauce version; salted rakkyo are generally not eaten on their own without aging, but some people enjoy them.

Salted Rakkyo

2 lbs (1 kg) rakkyo
⅔ oz (20 g) salt (2% of the weight of the rakkyo)

Container capacity: 8½ cups (2 liters)
Pickling time: 6 hours
Lifespan: 1 year refrigerated

1 Wash the rakkyo carefully. Remove the hairy roots, peel off the outer layer, and drain well. (If the rakkyo have been pre-washed, simply rinse them briefly.)
2 Put the rakkyo in a large bowl and sprinkle evenly with the salt. Leave for 8 hours at room temperature, then refrigerate until ready to make Sweet Vinegar Rakkyo or Soy Sauce Pickled Rakkyo.

Sweet Vinegar Rakkyo

7 oz (200 g) Salted Rakkyo
3 tablespoons sugar
½ cup (120 ml) rice vinegar
1 tablespoon plus 1 teaspoon water

Container capacity: 2 cups (500 ml)
Pickling time: 1 week
Lifespan: 1 year refrigerated

1 Drain the Salted Rakkyo and pat dry. Pack into jar. Whisk the sugar with the vinegar and water until dissolved and pour into the jar.

2 Cover with a lid and leave the jar at room temperature for 1 week. Store in the refrigerator to keep the crunchy texture.

Soy Sauce Pickled Rakkyo

1 lb (500 g) Soy Sauce Koji (page 33)
1 lb (500 g) Salted Rakkyo

Container capacity: 6½ cups (1.5 liters)
Pickling time: 1 month
Lifespan: 1 year refrigerated

1 Put about a third of the Soy Sauce Koji in the bottom of a jar. Drain the Salted Rakkyo and pat dry. Pack them into the jar.

2 Add the remaining Soy Sauce Koji and smooth the surface so that the rakkyo are completely covered. Put on the lid and leave for about a month at room temperature. Store in the refrigerator to keep the crunchy texture.

Pickled Garlic

Garlic—everyone's favorite aromatic—is wonderful when pickled, skin and all, in soy sauce or miso. It can be eaten as is, or grated or sliced to use as seasoning in various dishes. The garlic-flavored pickling liquid and pickling bed make wonderful seasonings as well! In the preliminary step, whole heads of garlic are soaked in the liquid produced in making classic Red Shiso Umeboshi (page 50). If you don't have any on hand, rice vinegar and salt may be used.

Vinegared Garlic

10 heads garlic
2½ cups (600 ml) white ume vinegar (step 2 on page 50), or
    1⅔ cups (400 ml) rice vinegar mixed with 1⅓ oz (40 g) salt

Container capacity: 6½ cups (1.5 liters)
Pickling time: 8 hours, plus one day to dry

1 Place the unpeeled garlic bulbs in a jar and pour the white ume vinegar over them. Let stand for 8 hours.

2 Remove the garlic bulbs from the liquid and put them on a wide flat sieve or on a rack. Dry in the sun for one entire day.

Garlic Preserved in Soy Sauce

9 oz (250 g) Vinegared Garlic (see above)
2 x 6 inch (5 x 15 cm) piece dried kombu seaweed
¾ cup (180 ml) dark soy sauce
4 tablespoons mirin

Container capacity: 4 cups (1 liter)
Pickling time: 3 months
Lifespan: 1 year refrigerated

1 Pack the vinegared garlic bulbs in a jar with the kombu seaweed. Add the soy sauce and mirin.

2 Cover with a lid and let stand at room temperature for 3 months. The garlic is ready when all the cloves have turned dark. Use the garlic soy sauce as a seasoning in other dishes.

Garlic Preserved in Miso

9 oz (250 g) Vinegared Garlic (see above)
9 oz (250 g) miso paste
½ cup (100 g) sugar

Container capacity: 4 cups (1 liter)
Pickling time: 3 months
Lifespan: 1 year refrigerated

1 Mix the sugar and miso together. Coat each head of vinegared garlic with this paste. Pack into a jar.

2 Cover with a lid and let stand at room temperature for 3 months. The garlic is ready when the miso flavor has permeated the cloves completely. Use the garlic miso as a seasoning in other dishes.

Potato Salad with Rakkyo

Pickled rakkyo are a great sweet-sour accent in creamy potato salad! Use the pickling vinegar instead of dressing to make a healthy version of this favorite, which is every bit as tasty.

Serves 2

2 medium potatoes, scrubbed but not peeled
A few Sweet Vinegar Rakkyo pickles (page 67), about 2 oz (50 g)
1 tablespoon pickling vinegar from Sweet Vinegar Rakkyo (page 67)

1 Prepare a steamer basket. Put the whole, unpeeled potatoes in and steam for about 15 minutes, or until tender.
2 Remove potatoes from the steamer and peel while still hot. Place in a bowl and mash coarsely with a fork.
3 Slice the rakkyo pickles into thin rounds and add to the potatoes along with the pickling vinegar. Mix well. Serve warm or cold.

Rakkyo Pickles with Natto

Natto (fermented soybeans) is often served with sliced green onion. Using rakkyo pickles instead adds a sour-sweet flavor. They are a superb complement to the natto—no other condiments are needed.

Serves 2

1 small package natto, about 2 oz (50 g)
1 bulb Sweet Vinegar Rakkyo pickle (page 67)

1 Slice the pickled rakkyo into very thin rounds.
2 Combine the rakkyo and the natto and mix thoroughly.

Pan-fried Garlic Pork

You don't need any additional sauce if you have some garlic preserved in soy sauce on hand. Just a little goes a long way with pork. The juices of the pork and the fragrance of the garlic are an irresistible combination.

Serves 2

Two ¾ inch (1.5 cm) thick slices pork shoulder
Salt and coarsely ground black pepper, to taste
½ clove Garlic Preserved in Soy Sauce (page 69)
¼ onion
2 fresh shiitake mushrooms
1 tablespoon rapeseed or canola oil
Watercress for garnish

1 Make several cuts into the line between the fat and meat of the pork. Salt and pepper both sides.
2 Peel the garlic and slice very thinly. Cut the onion into wedges. Remove the stems from the mushrooms.
3 Heat the oil in a skillet. Add the pork and brown on both sides. Scatter the garlic slices on top.
4 Transfer the pork to a serving dish. Use the same skillet to sauté the onion and shiitake mushrooms until tender. Serve alongside the pork and garnish with the watercress.

Garlic Miso Dip

The miso used to preserve the garlic, rather than the garlic itself, is used for this dip. This is fabulous with crudités—it's hard to stop eating them! You can thin out the miso with a little mirin or vinegar if you like.

Serves 2

2 tablespoons miso from Garlic Preserved in Miso (page 69)
Raw vegetables of your choice, such as daikon radish, carrots, cucumber, and celery

1 Peel the daikon radish and carrot and cut into sticks. Cut up the cucumber and celery in the same way so that they are as close to the same size as possible.
2 Scoop the miso into a small bowl and serve with the vegetables. Dip the vegetables into the miso to eat.

Sake Lees Pickles

Sake lees—the fermented crushed rice left over after sake has been pressed—are heady with the fragrance and flavor of sake. Letting vegetables ferment in a mixture of mature sake lees paste, salt and sugar creates wonderful pickles.

Sake Lees Pickled Vegetables

Piece daikon radish, about 5 oz (150 g)
2 small Asian eggplants, about 4½ oz (130 g) total
1 small Japanese cucumber or ½ large cucumber
2 myoga ginger buds
3 garlic cloves
1 teaspoon salt

FOR THE SAKE LEES PICKLING BED
2 lbs (1 kg) sake lees paste
1½ cups (300 g) sugar
1⅔ oz (50 g) salt

Container capacity: 12 cups (3 liters)
Pickling time: 6 hours
Lifespan: 3 days refrigerated

1 Cut the daikon radish into quarters lengthwise. Cut the cucumber in half lengthwise if small, or into quarters if large; remove seeds if needed. Peel and halve the garlic. Cut the eggplant in half lengthwise. Rub all the vegetables with the 1 teaspoon salt.

2 Let the salted vegetables stand for at least an hour to draw out excess moisture.

3 Make the sake lees pickling bed. Put the sake lees paste in a bowl. Add the sugar and salt in several batches, mixing well after each addition. When the paste is smooth, it's ready.

4 Pat the vegetables dry with a paper towel and bury them completely in the sake lees pickling bed.

5 Smooth out the surface and let stand for 6 hours. The pickles may be eaten right away or removed from the pickling bed and refrigerated. The pickling bed can be used several times. If it gets too wet, make fresh pickling-bed mixture and mix it in.

Ginger in Sake Lees

The intoxicating fragrance of the sake lees and the assertive fragrance of the ginger combine to make an irresistible pickle! Rub the salt in well at the start to draw out the moisture from the ginger.

5 pieces fresh ginger root, about 10 oz (300 g) total
1 teaspoon salt (2% of the weight of the ginger)
7 oz (200 g) Sake Lees Pickling Bed (recipe below)

FOR THE SAKE LEES PICKLING BED
14 oz (400 g) sake lees
⅔ cup (120 g) sugar
1 heaping tablespoon salt

Container capacity: 4 cups (1 liter)
Pickling time: 8 hours
Lifespan: 2 weeks in the refrigerator

1 Combine all the pickling bed ingredients and mix well.

*** The sake lees pickling bed can be used several times. If it gets too watery, mix up a new batch and add it to the old bed.**

2 Scrub each piece of ginger well. Rub the salt firmly into the surface.

3 Line the bottom of the container with a thin layer of the pickling-bed mixture. Arrange the ginger pieces in a single layer, leaving as few gaps as possible.

4 Add the remaining mixture, filling in any gaps between the ginger.
5 Smooth out the surface so the ginger is completely covered. Cover and leave at room temperature for 8 hours.

6 Store in the refrigerator until serving. To serve, wipe off the sake lees and slice the ginger thinly.

Enoki Mushrooms in Sake Lees

Serve these pickles with a little of the sake lees still clinging to the enoki mushrooms. The delightful texture comes from steaming the mushrooms briefly before pickling them.

Bunch of enoki mushrooms, roots removed, about 7 oz (200 g)
14 oz (400 g) Sake Lees Pickling Bed (page 72)

Container capacity: 4 cups (1 liter)
Pickling time: 1 hour
Lifespan: 5 days refrigerated

1 Set a steamer basket over water in a pan. Bring to a boil, add the enoki mushrooms, cover and steam for 5 minutes.
2 Line the bottom of the container with a thin layer of the sake lees mixture. Spread the enoki mushrooms on top and cover with the remaining mixture. Smooth out the top. Cover and let stand for 1 hour. Store in the refrigerator until serving. To serve, wipe off most of the sake lees and cut the mushrooms into bite-sized pieces.

Carrot Pickled in Sake Lees

These crunchy pickled carrots are sweet and fragrant.

1 carrot, about 7 oz (200 g)
⅔ teaspoon salt (2% of the weight of the carrot)
7 oz (200 g) Sake Lees Pickling Bed (page 72)

Container capacity: 4 cups (1 liter)
Pickling time: 8 hours
Lifespan: 1 week in the refrigerator

1 Peel the carrot. Cut in half lengthwise, then cut each half in two crosswise. Rub the salt into the carrot pieces.
2 Line the bottom of the container with a thin layer of the sake lees mixture and arrange the carrot pieces on top. Add the remaining mixture and smooth out the surface. Cover and let stand for 8 hours. To serve, wipe off the sake lees and cut the carrot into small pieces. Keep refrigerated.

Shibazuke Pickles

This is a classic summer vegetable pickle with eggplant, myoga ginger buds and shiso leaves pickled in salt. Even if you omit the red shiso leaves, the fermentation will turn the pickles a reddish-purple color, with a refreshing sour flavor. They can be eaten as is, or finely minced and as a seasoning or garnish for other dishes.

6 small Asian eggplants, about 14 oz (400 g) total
8 myoga ginger buds, about 12 oz (350 g) total
70 green shiso leaves, about 2 oz (50 g) total
⅞ oz (24 g) salt (3% of the total weight of the vegetables)

Container capacity: 12 cups (3 liters)
Pickling time: 3 to 4 days
Lifespan: 1 month refrigerated

1 Cut the eggplants in half length-wise, then slice diagonally. Cut the myoga ginger buds into eighths diagonally. Put half of the eggplant and myoga in a bowl.

2 Layer half the green shiso leaves on top of the vegetables in the bowl. Sprinkle half of the salt over all.

3 Add the rest of the eggplant and myoga ginger buds. Layer the remaining the shiso leaves over the vegetables and sprinkle with the rest of the salt.

4 Place a sturdy plate or wooden drop lid on top of the vegetables in the bowl and top with a 5½ pound (2.5 kg) weight. Let stand until the liquid exuded by the vegetables reaches the level of the drop lid, then reduce the weight by half. Let stand for another three to four days. When the vegetables have turned red-dish-purple and taste a bit sour, they are ready to eat. Store in the refrigerator.

Dried Daikon Pickles

Called *tsubozuke* in Japanese, these are old-fashioned pickles of sliced and dried daikon radish, soy sauce and mirin, pickled in a ceramic jar. They are crunchy and chewy, redolent with the umami of the soy sauce, and will become darker and more complex as they mature, so you can enjoy them for a long time.

½ small daikon radish, about 1 lb (500 g)
2 teaspoons salt (2% of the weight of the
** daikon radish)**
3 tablespoons plus 1 teaspoon dark soy sauce
2 tablespoons mirin
1 tablespoon sugar

Container capacity: 4 cups (1 liter)
Pickling time: 1 week
Lifespan: 1 year refrigerated

1 Quarter the unpeeled daikon radish and slice thinly.

2 Place the daikon radish slices in a bowl and sprinkle the salt over evenly. Let stand for 30 minutes, then firmly squeeze out any liquid.

3 Arrange the daikon radish slices in a single layer on a large, flat sieve or rack. Dry in the sun for about 6 hours. They don't have to dry out completely.

4 Transfer the dried daikon radish to a bowl. Add the soy sauce, mirin and sugar and mix well to combine.

5 Transfer to a container and let stand for 6 hours.

6 Set a 1 pound (500 g) weight on the radishes. Let the container stand at room temperature for 1 week. Store in the refrigerator.

Even More Reasons to Enjoy Pickles

Fermentation brings health and vitality

In my ongoing exploration of pickles, I'm constantly reminded how wonderful they are. Not only do they improve the flavor of the items that are pickled, but they also extend the length of time that they remain edible.

The fermentation process causes microorganisms such as bacteria, yeasts and molds to produce chemical changes in the foods being fermented. One such process is lactic acid fermentation, which brings about healthful changes to the ingredients. It is amazing that highly beneficial lactic acid bacteria can be produced simply by pickling vegetables in salt. It boosts the umami in the vegetables and adds a pleasantly sour flavor. The bacteria produced this way, called plant lactobacillus or plant-based lactic acid bacteria, is different from the lactic acid bacteria in yogurt and other dairy products.

What, then, is the difference between fermentation and decay? Both are the result of microorganisms in action, but fermentation results in foods that are good for us, while decay is harmful. In other words, the distinction between the two is purely arbitrary and centered around the needs of human beings. Beneficial microorganisms improve our digestive systems, making absorption and elimination more efficient, and also strengthen our immune systems—they're all-round good guys!

Rice-bran-pickled vegetables are more nutritious

Rice-bran pickling is also a type of lactic acid fermentation. Rice bran—the outer part of the grain and the germ that's removed by milling the rice—is rich in B vitamins and minerals. When salt is added to rice bran and vegetables are pickled in the mix, a large amount of lactic acid bacteria is produced in that pickling bed. Some of the nutrients in the rice bran are transferred to the vegetables during the pickling process, making them even more nutritious than before! The B vitamins in particular help reduce fatigue and are good for the skin. For these benefits, in addition to their great taste, making rice-bran pickles regularly is certainly worthwhile.

CHAPTER 3

Pickling with the Seasons

In spring I gather the wild shoots that peek out from under the dry, dead grass and pickle them. In summer I preserve lively aromatic herbs to capture the scents and flavors of the season. I take a break from pickling in the fall, but in the winter, vegetables like napa cabbage and daikon radish reach their peak, so I become busy with my pickling again. I also make long-keeping pickles such as salted *nozawana* greens and flavorful *takuan* pickles from whole daikon radishes. Pickling was originally devised as a way to prolong our enjoyment of seasonal bounty. Why not enjoy living in harmony with the changing seasons by making pickles?

It might be a challenge to find some of the vegetables and herbs used in this chapter, but they are available from specialty produce sites online. Some could even be grown in your garden!

Spring

Salt-pickled Butterbur

Use thin mountain butterbur (called *fuki* in Japanese) if you can get it, and do not peel or cut the stems. Pickle them in 30 percent salt for long-term preservation. These umami-rich pickles can be used as a seasoning.

1lb 3 oz (600 g) young butterbur stalks
6⅓ oz (180 g) salt (30% of the weight
of the butterbur)

Container capacity: 12 cups (3 liters)
Pickling time: About 1 month
Lifespan: 1 year at room temperature

1 Lay a third of the butterbur in the pickling container and sprinkle with a quarter of the salt. Repeat twice more, finishing with the remaining salt.

2 Set a 4½ pound (2 kg) weight on top of the salted butterbur and let stand at room temperature for 1 month.

3 Reduce the weight by half and cover with a lid. Store at room temperature. Before serving, soak in plain water for 6 hours to draw out some of the salt.

Serving suggestion
Because these pickles are so salty, soak them in water before eating. They can be cut up and simmered with deep-fried tofu (*atsuage*) or dried shredded daikon radish (*kiriboshi daikon*). They are also delicious chopped up and added to steamed sticky rice or to vinegared dishes.

Butterbur Sprouts with Kombu and Soy Sauce

The subtle flavor of butterbur sprouts is enhanced by pickling them in a mixture of soy sauce and kombu seaweed dashi stock. Take a bite and fill your senses with their wonderful fragrance!

5 oz (150 g) fresh butterbur sprouts
½ teaspoon salt (2% of the weight of the sprouts)
7 tablespoons soy sauce
⅓ oz (10 g) shredded dried kombu seaweed
7 tablespoons water

Container capacity: 4 cups (1 liter)
Pickling time: 2 to 3 days
Lifespan: 6 months refrigerated

1 Put the butterbur sprouts in a bowl. Sprinkle with the salt and mix by hand, squeezing well. Set a 1 pound (500 g) weight on top of the sprouts and let stand for 8 hours.

2 Drain the sprouts well, squeezing out the excess moisture. Transfer the butterbur sprouts to the pickling container and add the soy sauce.

3 Bring the kombu and water to a boil in a small pan. Add the kombu and water to the pickling container. Cover and let stand in a cool, dry place for two to three days. When the butterbur sprouts have taken on the color of the soy sauce, they are ready to eat.

Serving suggestion
These pickles can be eaten as is, but you can also mince them finely and combine it with other ingredients. Try serving mixed in with hot tofu or noodles, as a topping on plain rice or mixed into vegetable side dishes.

Salt-pickled Bracken

Like the Salt-pickled Butterbur on page 84, bracken shoots (called *warabi* in Japanese) are used in long uncut pieces and pickled in 30 percent salt. Soaking them in water before eating removes the bitterness, leaving delicious, umami-rich pickles that can be enjoyed all year round.

3 lbs (1.4 kg) bracken shoots
15 oz (420 g) salt (30% of the
  weight of the bracken shoots)

Container capacity: 12 cups (3 liters)
Pickling time: About 1 month
Lifespan: 1 year at room temperature

1 Arrange a third of the bracken shoots in the pickling container and sprinkle with a fourth of the salt.

2 Lay another third of the bracken crosswise over the first layer and top with another fourth of the salt. Repeat with the remaining bracken, finishing with the rest of the salt.

3 Place a sturdy lid directly on the bracken and set 9 pounds (4 kg) of weight on top. Let stand at room temperature for a month. Reduce the weight by half and cover with a lid. Store pickles at room temperature. Before serving, soak in plain water for 6 hours to draw out some of the salt.

Serving suggestion
Soak the bracken shoots in plain water to draw out some of the salt before eating. They can be cut up and served as a side dish or added to vinegared dishes. Pickled bracken simmered with dried sardines and tiny squid is a specialty of my home region of Shinshu.

Salt-pickled Water Celery

The water celery (*seri* in Japanese, also called Japanese parsley or water dropwort) is pickled in salt with the roots still attached. Crunchy and subtly bitter, it adds fragrance to many dishes.

Bunch of water celery, roots attached, about 12 oz (350 g)
2 teaspoons salt (3% of the weight of the water celery)

Container capacity: 8½ cups (2 liters)
Pickling time: 8 hours
Lifespan: 1 month refrigerated

 **1** Bend the water celery, with roots still attached, to fit in a container in a flat layer. Sprinkle evenly with the salt.

 **2** Place a lid directly on the water celery and set a 3½ pound (1.5 kg) weight on top. Let stand for 8 hours. When the water celery has released liquid and the stems are soft, it is ready. Transfer to a plastic storage bag and refrigerate.

Serving suggestion
Sprinkle this pickle on top of unsalted soup to add fragrance and savor. It can be used in egg-drop soup and rice porridge, too. Or chop it up and mix it with daikon radish or seafood—no need to add salt.

Wild Garlic Pickled in Soy Sauce

The pungency of wild garlic (*Allium macrostemon*) is transformed into umami by the soy sauce. Pickled this way, it makes a delicious seasoning.

Bunch of wild garlic, about 3½ oz (100 g)
7 tablespoons soy sauce

Container capacity: 2 cups (500 ml)
Pickling time: 8 hours
Lifespan: 1 month refrigerated

 **1** Cut the wild garlic into small pieces, keeping the white bulbs intact. Place in a bowl and swirl in the soy sauce. Mix well.

 2 Transfer the wild garlic and soy sauce to a container. Set a 1 pound (500 g) weight on top and let stand at room temperature for 8 hours. Store in the refrigerator.

Serving suggestion
This makes a nice accompaniment for drinks or rice. It's also tasty as a topping for steamed vegetables, or mixed into fried rice or other stir-fried dishes. Add to vinegar to make a dipping sauce for deep-fried foods.

Nanohana Pickled in Mustard

Nanohana, a close relative of broccoli or rapini, is harvested in spring. Use tender sprouting broccoli or broccolini if you can't find nanohana. The mustard-soy sauce it is pickled in tones down its bitterness and pungency greatly.

7 oz (200 g) nanohana or sprouting broccoli
½ teaspoon karashi mustard powder
2 tablespoons light (usukuchi) soy sauce

Container capacity: 2 cups (500 ml)
Pickling time: 8 hours
Lifespan: 3 days refrigerated

1 Blanch the nanohana in boiling water briefly, then drain and spread the florets out on a plate or tray. Mix the mustard and soy sauce together and drizzle over the nanohana.

2 Transfer to a container and set a 2 pound (1 kg) weight on top. Let stand for 8 hours. Store in the refrigerator.

Serving suggestion
Try mixing this into rice or serving on top of rice, or use it to season squid or white chicken dishes. It's also good with grilled fish or stir-fried dishes.

Nanohana with Kombu

Wrapping nanohana in kombu seaweed gives it lots of umami and rich flavor. It's a great way to preserve this tender vegetable.

14 oz (400 g) nanohana or sprouting broccoli
Splash of rice vinegar
6 x 12 in (13 x 30 cm) piece dried kombu seaweed
1 heaping teaspoon salt (2% of the weight of the nanohana)

Container capacity: 2 cups (500 ml)
Pickling time: 8 hours
Lifespan: 3 days if refrigerated

1 Blanch the nanohana in boiling water briefly, then drain. Moisten a cloth with a little rice vinegar and wipe down the kombu to soften it. Bend it into a U shape to fit into the container. Layer the nanohana on top while sprinkling with salt.

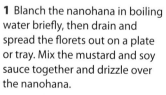

2 Fold the kombu up around the nanohana. Set a 2½ pound (1.2 kg) weight on top and let stand at room temperature for 8 hours, or until the nanohana has absorbed plenty of flavor. Store in the refrigerator.

Serving suggestion
Cut into small pieces and mix into rice, or add to chirashizushi (scattered sushi). Try it quickly stir-fried with canola oil, too.

Bamboo Shoots Pickled in Miso

Fresh bamboo shoots are a quintessential springtime vegetable in Japan. Preserving them in miso helps them keep longer, and enhances their umami and richness. They can be eaten just as they are—no need to wipe off the miso.

1 fresh young bamboo shoot, about 7 oz (200 g)
2 scant tablespoons miso paste

Pickling time: 3 hours
Lifespan: 5 days refrigerated

1 Cut the bamboo shoot into quarters lengthwise. Rub the miso into the cut sides.

2 Firmly stuff the miso into the crevices of the bamboo shoot as well.

3 Put the miso-coated pieces of bamboo shoot back together to form a whole piece again. Wrap in cling film and refrigerate for at least 3 hours. Cut into bite-sized pieces and eat as is, miso and all.

Serving suggestion
This pickle is delicious sliced and added to miso soup (reduce the amount of miso in the soup). Try simmering with deep-fried tofu pockets (abura-age) or adding to stir-fried dishes.

Summer

Sansho Peppercorns in Soy Sauce

Wash the sansho peppercorns well under running water. If you can't find sansho peppercorns, use regular green ones instead.

9 oz (250 g) fresh sansho peppercorns
1¼ cup (300 ml) soy sauce

Container capacity: 2½ cups (600 ml)
Pickling time: 1 week
Lifespan: 6 months refrigerated

1 Wash the sansho peppercorns well under running water. Place in a colander or in a sieve lined with a paper towel and pat dry.

2 Transfer to a container and add the soy sauce. Cover and refrigerate for one week. Refrigerate until serving.

Serving suggestion

Serve with cold noodles or chilled tofu, on top of grilled eel, or as a salty complement to sweet adzuki bean and mochi soup. Perfect when you want some fragrance and spiciness.

Sansho Peppercorns in Soy Sauce and Koji

Mixing the spicy sansho peppercorns with soy sauce and rice koji makes for a mild, well-rounded flavor, thanks to the power of fermentation!

7 oz (200 g) dry rice koji
1¼ cup (300 ml) soy sauce
3⅓ oz (100 g) fresh sansho peppercorns

Container capacity: 4 cups (1 liter)
Pickling time: 1 week
Lifespan: 6 months refrigerated

1 Three days ahead of time, make the soy-sauce rice koji. Crumble the rice koji into a bowl and add the soy sauce. Allow to ferment for about 3 days, stirring once or twice a day.
2 Wash the sansho peppercorns well in running water. Place in a colander or sieve lined with a paper towel and pat dry. In a bowl, combine the peppercorns and the soy sauce rice koji. Transfer to a container, cover and refrigerate for 1 week.

Serving suggestion
Eat as is or on top of plain rice. Serve with meat dishes or add as a seasoning to stir-fries for a boost of aroma and sweetness.

Sansho Peppercorns in Sake Lees

The sweet fragrance and deep flavor of the sake lees mellow out the pungency of the peppercorns. Try pan-roasting for an amazing fragrance.

9 oz (250 g) sake lees
5 tablespoons sugar
2 teaspoons salt
3½ oz (100 g) fresh sansho peppercorns

Container capacity: 3⅓ cups (800 ml)
Pickling time: 1 week
Lifespan: 6 months refrigerated

1 In a bowl, mix together the sake lees, sugar and salt to make the pickling bed.
2 Wash the peppercorns well in running water. Place in a colander or sieve lined with a kitchen towel, and pat dry. Mix the peppercorns into the sake lees pickling bed. Transfer to a container, cover and refrigerate for 1 week.

Serving suggestion
These are a great dip for vegetables. You can also roast them in a dry skillet and add to fish dishes, or brush them onto fish or meat before pan-frying or grilling. They are also an excellent general seasoning.

Sansho Peppercorns in Miso

Peppercorns go very well with miso, too. Mix with a slightly sweet miso bed and leave to mature. Try using this as a special seasoning!

7 oz (200 g) miso paste
3 tablespoons sugar
3½ oz (100 g) fresh sansho peppercorns

Container capacity: 2½ cups (600 ml)
Pickling time: 1 week
Lifespan: 6 months refrigerated

1 Mix the miso and sugar together to make the miso pickling bed. Wash the peppercorns well in running water. Place in a colander or sieve lined with a paper towel and pat dry. Stir the peppercorns into the miso mixture.
2 Transfer to a container, cover and refrigerate for 1 week.

Serving suggestion
These make a rich, flavorful sauce for grilled tofu. You can stir them into simple soups or add them to simmered dishes for greater depth of flavor.

Shiso Berries in Soy Sauce

The berries of the shiso plant have an interesting texture and an irresistible scent.

3½ oz (100 g) fresh shiso berries
7 tablespoons soy sauce

Container capacity: 2 cups (500 ml)
Pickling time: 1 week
Lifespan: 6 months refrigerated

1 Strip the berries from the shiso stems and put into a bowl. Wash well, drain and pat dry.

2 Pour the soy sauce into a container and add the shiso berries. Cover and refrigerate for one week. Keep refrigerated until serving.

Serving suggestion
Eat with hot plain rice, or as a topping on cold tofu. Mix with daikon radish, or sprinkle onto pickled napa cabbage as a flavor accent.

Shiso Leaves in Seasoned Vinegar and Soy Sauce

Green shiso leaves have a slightly minty fragrance. Here they are pickled in a mixture of seasoned vinegar and soy sauce.

70 green shiso leaves, about 2 oz (50 g)
½ tablespoon sugar
⅓ teaspoon salt
1 tablespoon rice vinegar
1 tablespoon plus 1 teaspoon water
7 tablespoons soy sauce

Container capacity: 2 cups (500 ml)
Pickling time: 1 hour
Lifespan: 6 months refrigerated

1 Layer the green shiso in the container about 10 leaves at a time. Whisk the sugar and salt with the rice vinegar and water, until dissolved.

2 Add the sweet vinegar and the soy sauce to the container, and put a 1 pound (500 g) weight on top to keep the shiso leaves submerged. Let stand for an hour, then store in the refrigerator.

Serving suggestion
Spread out the leaves and wrap them around plain rice or *onigiri* rice balls. Shred finely and mix into rice, or mince and use as a seasoning in other dishes.

Young Ginger with Red Shiso

Young ginger is dyed with red shiso leaves to make a classic condiment called *beni-shoga* (red pickled ginger). Use thin-skinned, tender young ginger. If you can't find red shiso leaves, they are easy to grow from seed.

2 lbs (1 kg) young ginger root
⅔ oz (20 g) salt (2% of the weight of the ginger)
1 additional tablespoon salt
7 oz (200 g) red shiso leaves
3⅓ cups (800 ml) Sa Shi Su ume vinegar (page 47)

* If you don't have Sa Shi Su ume vinegar, substitute sweet vinegar: mix together 2½ cups (600 ml) rice vinegar, ¾ cup (150 g) sugar, and ½ oz (15 g) salt.

Container capacity: 8½ cups (2 liters)
Pickling time: 24 hours, plus 1 to 2 weeks
Lifespan: 1 year at room temperature

1 Break the ginger root into single sections and wash without peeling. Drain and pat dry. Put the ginger root in a bowl and sprinkle with the salt. Toss to distribute well.

2 Set a 2 pound (1 kg) weight directly on the ginger and let stand at room temperature for 8 hours, then squeeze out the excess moisture. Repeat this process two more times.

3 Arrange the red shiso leaves and ginger root in alternating layers in a jar. Pour the Sa Shi Su ume vinegar over. Cover and leave at room temperature for 1 to 2 weeks. When the ginger turns red, the pickles are ready.

Serving suggestion
Use in sushi rolls, inarizushi (fried tofu pockets stuffed with sushi rice), and as a topping on yakisoba noodles. Try mixing with other pickles to add some zing.

Mixed Vegetable Pickles

Fukujinzuke, which means "lucky god pickles," is a luxurious mix of pickled roots and summer vegetables. The ingredients are pickled in salt, then dried and pickled in a seasoned liquid. You can enjoy multiple textures and flavors in this one pickle.

Piece daikon radish, about
   7 oz (200 g)
1 segment lotus root, about 5 oz
   (150 g)
1 carrot, about 5 oz (150 g)
2 small Asian eggplants, about
   3½ oz (100 g) total
1 small or ½ large cucumber, about
   3½ oz (100 g) total
3 myoga ginger buds
2 small green bell peppers
4 cups (1 liter) water
1 oz (30 g) salt
7 tablespoons rice vinegar
7 tablespoons soy sauce
4 tablespoons mirin
2⅓ teaspoons sugar

Container capacity: 4 cups (1 liter)
Pickling time: 30 minutes
Lifespan: 10 days refrigerated

1 Quarter the radish, lotus root, carrot, and eggplants lengthwise, then slice. Slice the cucumber. Halve the myoga ginger buds lengthwise. Core the bell peppers and slice into rounds. Put all the vegetables in a bowl. Mix the salt and water and pour over. Let stand for 1 hour, then drain and squeeze out well. Dry on a large flat sieve or rack in the sun for 2 to 3 hours.

2 Put the dried vegetables in a bowl. Add the vinegar and mix well, then drain and squeeze out the excess moisture again.

3 Transfer the vegetables to a container and add the soy sauce, mirin and sugar. Mix well. Cover and let stand at room temperature for 30 minutes until the flavors have blended. Store in the refrigerator, mixing up from the bottom occasionally.

Serving suggestion
Fukujinzuke is a classic accompaniment for Japanese curry. These pickles can also be mixed into rice, or into mashed tofu with ground sesame seeds to make a dish called *shira-ae*. Try adding them to greens or lettuce to enhance a salad.

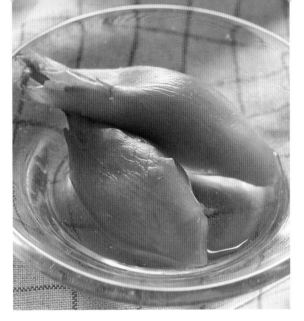

Myoga Ginger in Mustard

If you can find myoga ginger buds at your Japanese grocery store, this is a delicious pickle to make. Mustard powder is dissolved into the sweet seasoning liquid that's used to pickle the myoga ginger, giving it a pungent and appetizing flavor.

1 lb (500 g) fresh myoga ginger buds
½ oz (15 g) salt (3% of the weight of the myoga)
⅔ oz (20 g) mustard powder
6½ tablespoons sugar, about 2⅔ oz (80 g)
3 tablespoons plus 1 teaspoon sake
2 tablespoons plus 2 teaspoons rice vinegar

Container capacity: 8½ cups (2 liters)
Pickling time: 8 hours plus 3 days
Lifespan: 6 months refrigerated

1 Sprinkle the myoga ginger buds with the salt and let stand for an hour, then squeeze out well. Whisk the mustard powder, sugar, sake and vinegar together until the sugar is dissolved. Add to the salted myoga and mix well.
2 Put a sturdy plate or lid directly on the myoga ginger buds and set a 3½ pound (1.5 kg) weight on top for 8 hours. Transfer the myoga ginger to a container. Cover and let stand for 3 days.

Serving suggestion
Slice thinly and mix with summer vegetables to make a salad or side dish. Mince and use as a topping on cold tofu or boiled vegetables. Use as a seasoning in mixed rice or stir-fries.

Myoga Ginger in Sweet Vinegar

Myoga ginger buds have a mildly pungent flavor. Pickling in vinegar gives them an addictive crunchy-crispy texture and turns the buds a pretty red color. This pickle lasts for a long time, so it's well worth making to add to your stock!

10 oz (300 g) fresh myoga ginger buds
⅓ cup (75 ml) rice vinegar
2½ tablespoons sugar
1 teaspoon salt
7 tablespoons water

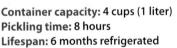
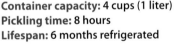

Container capacity: 4 cups (1 liter)
Pickling time: 8 hours
Lifespan: 6 months refrigerated

1 Blanch the myoga ginger buds in boiling water for 30 seconds, then drain and transfer to a bowl. Add the vinegar while still hot. Stir in the sugar, salt and water and mix well. The myoga will turn red after a while.
2 Transfer to a container and cover. Refrigerate for 8 hours.

Serving suggestion
Cut the buds in half and use as a topping for sushi. Shred thinly and add to vinegared dishes, or slice into rounds and serve on top of cold tofu or natto (fermented soybeans).

Chrysanthemum Petals in Sweet Vinegar

Edible chrysanthemum petals, a popular fall garnish in Japan, lose their distinctive odor when they are pickled in sweet vinegar. The color remains vibrant, however, offering a nice contrast to many dishes.

3½ oz (100 g) edible chrysanthemum flowers

FOR THE SWEET VINEGAR
2 tablespoons rice vinegar
2 tablespoons plus 1 teaspoon water
1 tablespoon sugar
1 teaspoon salt

Container capacity: 1¼ cups (300 ml)
Pickling time: 1 hour
Lifespan: 1 week refrigerated

1 Remove the petals from the flowers. Blanch the petals very briefly in boiling water. Drain and cool in running water. Drain again and squeeze out tightly.

2 Put the petals in a container. Whisk all sweet vinegar ingredients and pour over. Cover and refrigerate for 1 hour.

Serving suggestion
Add to mixed sushi, salads, vinegared dishes or grilled fish.

Wasabi Leaves in Dashi Stock

Wasabi leaves and stems are pickled in a dashi stock made from dried sardines and soy sauce. If you can find fresh wasabi leaves, don't skip these pickles.

7 oz (200 g) fresh wasabi leaves
1 tablespoon sugar
¾ cup (200 ml) water
3–4 dried sardines (niboshi)
3 tablespoons plus 1 teaspoon mirin
3 tablespoons plus 1 teaspoon light (usukuchi) soy sauce

Container capacity: 2 cups (500 ml)
Pickling time: 1 hour
Lifespan: 5 days refrigerated

1 Cut the leaves into 1 inch (2.5 cm) pieces. Pick off the flowers and put both the leaves and flowers in a bowl. Add the sugar and massage to bring out the fragrance.

2 Bring the water and sardines to a boil in a small pan. Add the mirin and soy sauce. Pour this mixture over the leaves and flowers. Transfer to a container and leave for 1 hour at room temperature. Store in the refrigerator.

Serving suggestion
Serve with sashimi or grilled fish, add to vinegared seafood dishes, or serve on top of plain rice.

Fall and Winter

Yuzu-miso Persimmons

You can find dried persimmons at Japanese grocery stores and online. With the added richness of miso and the fragrance of yuzu citrus, these are meltingly delicious. Try them as a snack with green tea instead of traditional sweets!

**2 whole dried persimmons,
    about 3½ oz (100 g) total**
2 teaspoons miso paste
1 in (2.5 cm) yuzu zest

Pickling time: 8 hours
**Lifespan: 2 weeks at room
    temperature**

1 Cut the calyxes off the persimmons, and make a vertical slit in the fruit. Open and remove the seeds.

2 Spread miso on the inside of a persimmon. Top with yuzu peel and roll up the fruit. Repeat with the other persimmon.

3 Wrap the persimmons in cling film, neaten up their shapes and let stand at room temperature for 8 hours. Cut into bite-sized pieces to serve.

Serving suggestion
Slice thinly and sandwich between slices of raw daikon radish to make a tasty appetizer to serve with drinks. Mince finely and add to vegetable dishes or salads. Chop and add to simmered fish dishes for a little extra sweetness.

Beets Pickled in Honey

Marinating grated beet in honey eliminates its rather earthy odor and turns it into a smooth jam-like paste. This adds lots of color to a meal.

1 beet, about 7 oz (200 g)
3 tablespoons honey
1 tablespoon lemon juice

Container capacity: 1¼ cups (300 ml)
Pickling time: 1 hour
Lifespan: 2 weeks refrigerated

1 Peel the beet and grate it.

2 Put the honey and grated beet in a pan over a low flame. Heat slowly, stirring constantly, until cooked to your desired degree of softness. Add lemon juice at the end.

3 Transfer to a container and let stand for an hour at room temperature. The pickled beet is ready to eat when the flavors have mingled. Store in the refrigerator.

Serving suggestion
Spread like jam on bread or cake, or make sandwiches with it. Try using this pickle as a chutney with curries to add a sweet flavor.

Turnips in Sweet Vinegar

These pickled turnips are inspired by a traditional pickle called "one thousand leaf pickled turnips." Be sure to use large, mild Asian turnips, and slice them very thinly. Sliced and quickly blanched lotus roots or carrots can be pickled in the same way.

2 large Asian turnips, about 10 oz (300 g) total
1 teaspoon salt (2% of the weight of the turnips)

FOR THE SWEET VINEGAR
1 tablespoon rice vinegar
1 tablespoon plus 1 teaspoon water
½ tablespoon sugar
⅓ teaspoon salt
Zest of ½ yuzu fruit, slivered

Container capacity: 2 cups (500 ml)
Pickling time: 1 hour
Lifespan: 10 days refrigerated

1 Wash the turnips, but do not peel them. Cut off all but a short length of the turnip greens. Slice the turnips on a mandoline.

2 Sprinkle the sliced turnip on both sides with the salt. Let stand for 30 minutes. When they exude moisture, squeeze them out tightly. Whisk all sweet vinegar ingredients together.

3 Place a sliver of yuzu zest on a slice of turnip and fold in half. Repeat with the remaining yuzu zest and turnip slices. Arrange in a container, pour the sweet vinegar over and let stand for 1 hour. Store in the refrigerator.

Serving suggestion
Serve as is or sandwich in between slices of sashimi. Serve alongside plain rice or onigiri rice balls, or chop up and add to salad.

CHAPTER 4

Traditional Pickling

One of my most important pickling jobs of the year is putting
up certain pickles in very large quantities,
just as the Japanese always used to in the olden days.
The vegetables I particularly like to pickle in large quantities
are daikon radish, winter melon, and mustard greens.

In this chapter I'll also show you a traditional pickling recipe
using the red turnips that are a specialty of the region
of Japan I come from.

Takuan Pickled Daikon Radish

The iconic pickle known as *takuanzuke* is traditionally made with dried daikon radish. Recently, however, I tried making it with some smaller, firmer varieties of daikon that grow here in my home region of Shinshu, such as *togakure* and *koshin* (a red daikon radish), without drying them. The pickling base is a mixture of rice bran, salt and sugar, with kombu seaweed and red chili peppers. To this I added some dried eggplant leaves and persimmon skins for flavor and sweetness. I also added some Jerusalem artichokes to the pickling bed with the daikon radish, since they are purported to lower blood sugar levels and I enjoy their crunchy texture. These subtly sour pickles are said make your digestive system healthy, and if you serve them with green tea you won't be able to stop nibbling them! Make these pickles in early December to enjoy them from New Year through early summer. You can freeze these pickles right in the pickling bed to prolong their life.

22 lbs (10 kg) small, hard white daikon radishes
13 lbs (6 kg) red daikon radishes
9 lbs (4 kg) Jerusalem artichokes
9 lbs (4 kg) fresh or dry-roasted rice bran
3½ lbs (1.5 kg) salt
5½ lbs (2.5 kg) sugar
3½ oz (100 g) dried eggplant leaves
14 oz (400 g) dried persimmon peel
20 small red chili peppers
10 pieces dried kombu seaweed, each 2 inches (5 cm) square

Container capacity: 8 gallons (30 liters)
Pickling time: 15 days plus 1 month
Lifespan: 6 months in a cool, dark place

1 Wash the daikon radishes and Jerusalem artichokes thoroughly and drain on a large sieve or colander. Leave the smaller red daikon radishes whole; cut the bigger ones in half.

2 Put a layer of rice bran on the bottom of the pickling container, and sprinkle some of the salt over. Add a layer of daikon radishes, making sure they don't overlap.

3 Add a quarter of the remaining rice bran, then one fourth of the remaining salt and sugar. Add another layer of daikon radishes, then another fourth of the rice bran, salt and sugar.

4 Scatter half of the dried eggplant leaves, dried persimmon peel and red chili peppers on top. Layer in the kombu seaweed pieces. Add another fourth of the rice bran, salt and sugar.

5 Add the Jerusalem artichokes in a single layer, then add the last of the rice bran, salt and sugar.

6 Add the remaining daikon radishes, then the rest of the dried eggplant leaves, dried persimmon peel and red chili peppers, so that they cover everything.

7 Set two or three weights totaling about 130 pounds (60 kg) directly on the radishes. Let stand for 15 days, until the liquid from the vegetables rises up. Reduce the weights to 65 pounds (30 kg) and allow to mature for another month.

Narazuke Pickled Melon

The sake lees pickles called *narazuke* come from the city of Nara, which is famous for its sake. Because the Shinshu region has many clear streams, there are numerous sake breweries here as well. Sake lees being readily available, I often use them to make narazuke. I buy freshly harvested pickling melons (called *shirouri*, "white melons" in Japanese) in the summer, cut them in half, scoop out the seeds and pre-salt the flesh. This draws out the excess moisture so that the flavor of the sake lees penetrates more readily. The main pickling process is done in a ceramic or enameled jar, which keeps the alcohol in the sake from evaporating. The melons are first packed with sake lees; they are then placed cut side down in the pickling jar. In two weeks the fresh, crunchy narazuke are ready to eat. The pickles will become darker in color and more fragrant the longer you let them mature.

31 lbs (14 kg) Asian pickling melons (available at Asian grocery stores)
3 lbs (1.4 kg) salt (10% of the weight of the melons, for the pre-salting)
22 lbs (10 kg) sake lees
2⅔ lbs (1.2 kg) sugar
3 oz (90 g) salt (for the main pickling)

Container capacity: about 4¾ gallons (18 liters)
Pickling time: 2 weeks to 1 month
Lifespan: 1 year in a cool, dark place

PRELIMINARY STEPS

1 Cut off both ends of each melon and cut in half lengthwise.
2 Scoop out the seeds and pith with a spoon.

PRE-SALTING

1 Rub the salt for pre-salting into the cavity of each melon and on the cut surface.
2 Arrange the melon pieces in the pickling container on their sides in the same direction.
3 When all the melon pieces have been packed in, sprinkle the top with the remaining salt. It's fine if some stick out of the container, as they will be pressed down by the weight.
4 Place a sturdy lid directly on the melons and set an 88 pound (40 kg) weight on top. In a day or so the moisture exuded from the melons will be visible. Proceed to main pickling at this point.

MAIN PICKLING

1 Take the melon pieces out, wipe them dry with a clean cloth and transfer to a bowl.
2 Mix the sake lees, sugar and the 3 oz salt together to make the pickling bed. Line the bottom of the container with some of the mixture. Fill the cavity of each melon with the sake lees mixture, then pack them cut side down into the container, along with additional pickling bed.
3 When all the melon pieces are packed in, cover the top with the remaining pickling bed and smooth it over.
4 Cover the container with a piece of parchment paper and secure with a piece of string. Store in a cool, dry place. You can start eating the narazuke after 2 weeks, but they will reach their full flavor after a month.

Nozawazuke Salt-pickled Mustard Greens

Although *nozawazuke* is known as a specialty pickle from the Shinshu region, it is actually made with the dark leafy *nozawa* greens (a type of mustard green) from the hot-springs village of Nozawa in northern Nagano prefecture. I grew up calling this pickle *o-happa*, which just means "leaves." Other traditional greens are also pickled in this region in the same way. Nozawa greens taste better if they have been through some frosty weather, so the main pickling is done in early December. Every winter I make two to three barrels of these pickles—each barrel is 20 kilograms, or about 44 pounds. I start by washing the barrels, then I wash the greens, and then I pickle them. It's an immense job, but when I think of the delicious pickles that will be produced at the end, my heart sings with joy. As the pickles mature over time, the dark green color gradually changes to a reddish brown, and the fermented flavor intensifies. Part of the fun of nozawazuke is observing how the flavor changes from the winter to the spring.

44 lbs (20 kg) nozawa greens or other mustard greens
1⅔ cups (400 ml) vinegar, for rinsing the pickling barrel
1 lb 3 oz (600 g) salt (3% of the weight of the greens)
1½ oz (40 g) red chili peppers

Container capacity: about 9½ gallons (36 liters)
Pickling time: about 17 days
Lifespan: 6 months in a cool, dark place

PREPARATORY STEPS

1 Fill a large bucket with water and wash the greens.
2 Spread out the leaves near the root ends and wash out the dirt thoroughly.
3 Rinse the barrel with vinegar to disinfect it.

PICKLING

1 The roots of nozawa greens are rather tough, so make a crisscross cut into the base of each bunch to ensure even pickling.
2 Pack some of the greens in the bottom of the barrel, alternating the leaf and root ends, and sprinkle with an appropriate portion of the salt. Scatter some of the chili peppers on top. Add another layer of greens, laying them crosswise over the first layer, then sprinkle with an additional portion of salt and chili peppers.
3 Keep on packing in layers of greens, salting each layer. Repeat until all the greens are packed in the barrel.
4 When all the greens have been added, press down hard on them with all your weight.
5 Add a generous amount of salt to finish, and sprinkle in the remaining red chili peppers.
6 Flatten out the surface and place a sturdy lid directly on the greens.
7 Set a 130 pound (60 kg) weight on top. After about a week, the moisture from the greens will be visible. Reduce the weight by half and leave for at least 10 more days. The pickles will now be ready to eat, and will continue to mature with time.

Sunkizuke Pickled Red Turnip Greens

Known as *sunkizuke* in Japanese, these are traditional pickles from the Kiso Valley at the foot of Mount Ontake in Nagano prefecture. They have a pleasant sourness and a unique fermented flavor. Instead of salt, they are pickled with a lactic-acid fermentation process initiated by a "mother" sunki-zuke made at an earlier time. Sunkizuke are traditionally made with the greens of a particular type of red turnip that grows in the region. For this book, I consulted with sunkizuke expert Hiroko Noguchi, who kindly shared this recipe with me. The turnip greens are first chopped up finely and doused quickly in boiling water, then put into a plastic bag with the "mother" sunkizuke pickles and left in a warm place for a day. The flavor is determined by the temperature of the pickles within 30 minutes of the time when these ingredients are combined, so make sure they don't get too cold or too warm. It's said that just 1 milliliter of the liquid from sunkizuke contains 100 million lactic acid bacteria. This fact made me really appreciate the power of these pickles. They're a healthy and nutritious food that is free of salt and rich in fiber.

6½ lbs (3 kg) red turnip greens
10 oz (300 g) sunkizuke pickles from an
earlier batch

Container capacity: 2½ gallons (10 liters)
Pickling time: About 3 days
Lifespan: 6 months in a cool, dark place

1 Separate the leaves and stems. Cut the leaves
into ½ to ¾ inch (1.5 to 2 cm) long pieces.
2 Chop up the stems and place them in a colander with the cut leaves.
3 Heat 2½ gallons (10 liters) of water to
between 140 and 158°F (60–70°C). Add the
chopped stems and leaves, let stand briefly,
then drain.
4 Put a large plastic bag in a Styrofoam box and
add the blanched greens.
5 Add the previously made sunkizuke pickles to
the bag and mix to incorporate.
6 Close up the plastic bag, cover the Styrofoam
box and leave for 24 hours so that the greens
in the bag ferment. The pickles will be ready in
about 3 days.

* Kiso is a cold region, so the sunkizuke pickles do
not need to be refrigerated until spring.

* The lactic acid bacteria in the sunkizuke
pickles are a mixture of those that ferment at a
temperature between 113 and 114°F (44–45°C)
and those that ferment at a lower temperature.
When they are done, they will contain more than
20 different kinds of lactic acid bacteria.

* The turnips themselves can be pickled in rice
bran or sweet vinegar.

* For authentic sunkizuke, you will probably have
to grow your own turnips. This variety is sown in
late August to September and grown in the field.
If you want to pickle them in winter, grow them
in a greenhouse and harvest them from the end
of October to mid-January. After harvesting the
turnips, cut off the greens and store the roots
separately.

Index of Recipes by Main Ingredient

"Books to Span the East and West"

Tuttle Publishing was founded in 1832 in the small New England town of Rutland, Vermont [USA]. Our core values remain as strong today as they were then—to publish best-in-class books which bring people together one page at a time. In 1948, we established a publishing office in Japan—and Tuttle is now a leader in publishing English-language books about the arts, languages and cultures of Asia. The world has become a much smaller place today and Asia's economic and cultural influence has grown. Yet the need for meaningful dialogue and information about this diverse region has never been greater. Over the past seven decades, Tuttle has published thousands of books on subjects ranging from martial arts and paper crafts to language learning and literature—and our talented authors, illustrators, designers and photographers have won many prestigious awards. We welcome you to explore the wealth of information available on Asia at **www.tuttlepublishing.com**.

Published by Tuttle Publishing, an imprint of Periplus Editions (HK) Ltd.

www.tuttlepublishing.com

YOKOYAMA TAKAKO NO OTSUKEMONO
Copyright © 2020 Takako Yokoyama
English translation rights arranged with SHUFU-TO-SEIKATSUSHA, LTD. through Japan UNI Agency, Inc., Tokyo

English translation by Makiko Itoh. English translation copyright © 2022 Periplus Editions (HK) Ltd.

ISBN: 978-4-8053-1663-4

24 23 22 21
10 9 8 7 6 5 4 3 2 1

Printed in China
2109EP

TUTTLE PUBLISHING® is a registered trademark of Tuttle Publishing, a division of Periplus Editions (HK) Ltd.

Distributed by

North America, Latin America & Europe
Tuttle Publishing
364 Innovation Drive
North Clarendon, VT 05759-9436 U.S.A.
Tel: 1 (802) 773-8930
Fax: 1 (802) 773-6993
info@tuttlepublishing.com
www.tuttlepublishing.com

Japan
Tuttle Publishing
Yaekari Building 3rd Floor
5-4-12 Osaki
Shinagawa-ku
Tokyo 141-0032
Tel: (81) 3 5437-0171
Fax: (81) 3 5437-0755
sales@tuttle.co.jp
www.tuttle.co.jp

Asia Pacific
Berkeley Books Pte. Ltd.
3 Kallang Sector #04-01
Singapore 349278
Tel: (65) 6741 2178
Fax: (65) 6741 2179
inquiries@periplus.com.sg
www.tuttlepublishing.com